The Man Who Would Be President

By
Cary Leiter

To my darling Chantal who will always remain to me
l'Amour De Ma Vie

TABLE OF CONTENTS

Part I:
The Beginning

1

He walked into the shabby hotel in Chelsea, trying to hide the look of distaste on his face. The dregs of society were gathered in the careworn lobby, passing the time by simply existing. They lay strewn around the large room, looking as if they were waiting to die without knowing it. He treated such people with disdain. He turned away from them, willing them to go away. They were not his problem.

Instead of going to the front desk, he headed quickly for the elevators, knowing very well what room he was supposed to go to. He was wearing a Mets windbreaker, which did not conceal his considerable girth, and a Mets cap, which somewhat concealed his monstrous comb-over. He thought his cap and windbreaker would throw any curiosity seekers off because he was known far and wide in New York as a Yankees fan.

He pressed the UP button and waited in front of the elevators for one of the cars to come down. As he stood there, looking ahead, ignoring the ignominious behavior around him, he wondered why they had wanted a meeting in such a slovenly place.

He had known the two people he was to meet for many years now; he had even contributed to the wife's campaign for the Senate.

They were probably after him for more money, he thought, and he would give it to them if need be, but anything more than that was not something he would agree to.

The car to his left opened first, and he was about to go inside when he saw an old lady with a disgruntled look coming out. So, he stepped aside to give her room to exit, and she moved slowly but surely out of the car and headed straight for the lobby. He didn't watch her progress because he was disgusted by old people, even though he was in his 70s; early 70s to be exact, but 70s nonetheless.

He stepped into the car and pressed the button for the fifth floor. It took a small eternity for the doors to close, and he was forced to look out onto the dinginess of the lobby while he waited, but eventually the doors slowly – much too slowly – came together, and he was alone as the car began to ascend – slowly and somewhat shakily. That's all he needed, he thought, to be crushed to death in an elevator accident in a shitbag of a hotel. That's all his enemies needed to hear. He would never live it down, even in death. He chuckled to himself – he had a bad sense of humor – and watched as the floor lights flashed on and off. At least something worked in that hotel from hell, a place he was looking forward to leaving as soon as possible.

When the elevator arrived on the fifth floor, he stepped out and tried to orient himself by looking at the signs announcing the room numbers. He turned to the left because that was where the room he was looking for would be. He tried his best not to look down at the ripped and filthy carpet he was walking on. The place disgusted him. After his business was concluded, he would never want to see it again. How can anybody live like this? he wondered. They have no one to blame but themselves for having no ambition. For not getting a good job and raising themselves above their stations. The dregs of society was right, he thought. They belong where they are because they didn't try to do anything about it. If it was up to him, he'd put them out of their misery; he'd execute them all. (Of course, he didn't take into consideration that as a child he had lived a very privileged life, and on his father's death, he inherited a goodly sum.)

It was at this fortuitous moment that he arrived in front of the door for Room 525. Its painting was chipped, and the numbers on the door were loose and almost swayed in the soft wind that blew through the hallway. That had to be their air conditioning, he thought, just as inferior as everything else in the building. He didn't want to touch the wood of the door with his hand, so he knocked with his foot.

After a moment, the door swung wide and revealed the host of this shindig, he supposed, Robert Borstrand. A fit man, a shade older than his guest, with a shock of white thick hair which did not need any kind of a combover, Bobby Borstrand smiled and held out his hand.

"Ed," he said, "Eddie. Good to see you. I hope you didn't have any trouble finding the place."

"No," Eddie said, "but I wish I had."

"Yeah," Borstrand agreed, "it is a bit of a mess, but that's why Julie chose it. Won't you come in?"

He stepped aside to let Edward (Eddie) Rowland cross the threshold.

"This is what is called a suite," Borstrand told him.

Rowland looked around him with as much distaste as he had when he first entered the lobby. They were in the front hallway, which just about fit the two of them. Borstrand led Rowland into the living room, if you could call it that. Its furniture was obviously second-hand, and its paint job was a puce green, or as Rowland would say, a puke green.

Sitting on the over-stuffed couch was Julie Reynolds Borstrand, former first lady of the country and senator of New York. She was instrumental in helping her husband gain the White House, in spite of their marital difficulties, because she had ambitions herself. She wanted to become president, but the republicans had a different idea. From the first moment she stepped into the White House, they started throwing everything they could find at her until her reputation suffered greatly. They knew what she wanted to become, and they were adamant about standing in her way.

However, she was a woman with brass balls, as one might say, and she never let anyone or anything stand in her way, especially not the Republican Party. They were the enemy, and she was there to save the country, if not the world, but many people thought she was too much of a Hawk who would get us into another war, on top of the one we had waged in Iraq, and the one in Afghanistan, which continued to rage, continually putting young men in danger. Her ambitions were thought to be unladylike by the republicans and that she should remain in the kitchen and the bedroom, in spite of the fact that there was not much activity going on in the bedroom anymore. Her focus was on the White House, and that is why she had brought Eddie Rowland in to see her. She was keeping this meeting a deep, dark secret, which befuddled Rowland, who was not much of a brain to begin with.

She held her hand out, and he took it reluctantly.

"Eddie," she said warmly, with a convincing smile, "how nice to see you."

"Nice to see you, too, Julie," he responded cautiously.

"Won't you please sit down?"

"Sure."

He sat in an armchair across from her.

"Bobby," Julie said to her husband, "why don't you make us some drinks?"

"Nothing for me," Rowland said, "I need my wits about me."

"Why's that?" asked Borstrand suspiciously.

"I don't know why you've called me here, and it makes me uncomfortable."

Borstrand moved to the wet bar in the corner as he said, "Nothing to be uncomfortable about. We're here to just have a nice chat."

He started mixing his wife's signature dry martini.

"Is that so?" said Rowland. "Then why are we in this shithole?"

Julie laughed and said, "Privacy, Eddie," smoothly. "Simple

privacy."

Rowland still wasn't convinced.

Borstrand moved to his wife and handed her her drink. "There you are, my dear," he said with a smile.

"Thank you, Bobby dear." And she took a sip of her drink. "Excellent, as usual," she complimented him.

"I'm glad you like it," Borstrand responded.

Rowland snickered in spite of himself. "What's all the lovey-dovey business for? You know you can act yourselves in front of me."

"Of course we do, Eddie," Julie said, "but we have to discuss a matter of great importance."

"Aha," Rowland exclaimed. "Now we get to it."

"What?" Julie asked innocently.

"Don't be that way with me, Julie," Rowland said, "we've known each other too long."

"So we have," Julie said. "Then we'll get straight to the point. Bobby?" She took a bigger sip of her drink this time.

Borstrand returned to the bar where he proceeded to fix himself a martini. "Eddie," he began, "as you well know, Julie is running for president."

"Yeah, that's right, she's pretty much got the nomination locked up."

"So she has, but we need some help on the other side."

"What's that got to do with me?" Eddie demanded.

"A great deal," Julie chimed in. "Just sit back and let Bobby do the talking."

Rowland didn't like to be told to shut up, even in the politest of terms, but this time he sat back and decided to listen.

"Now," Borstrand went on, "you know she has some stiff competition from the republicans. Primarily, Bud Congreve. Wouldn't you say he's the one she has to look out for?"

He kept silent and nodded.

"Good," Borstrand said. "That's where you come in. We want you to run for president on the republican ticket."

Rowland could no longer contain himself. He stood and said, "What the hell is this all about? I'm a Democrat and I've always been a Democrat."

Julie smiled and said, "Calm yourself, Eddie," with a reassuring smile. "All will be explained."

Having taken the wind out of his sails, Rowland sat back down and crossed his arms. His body language said he was not happy.

"Go on, Bobby," Julie said to her husband.

Borstrand raised his glass to Rowland. "The King is dead, Eddie. Long live the King."

"Now what the hell is that supposed to mean?" Rowland demanded to know.

"From here on out," Borstrand continued, "you will no longer be a Democrat. If you decide to help us, you will become a republican."

"But that's ridiculous," Rowland protested. "Everybody in this city knows I'm a Democrat. Why, I even contributed to your run for the Senate, Julie."

"That's true," Julie said sagely, "but you wouldn't be the first person to change your allegiance. You're disgusted with the way things are being handled in Washington, so you want to drain the swamp."

"That's a catchy way of putting it," Rowland conceded, "but people who know me best won't believe a word of it."

"Then you must convince them," Borstrand said. "Remember, this must remain our little secret. No one else must know about it."

"But this is not a simple little secret," Rowland said. "This is a fucking outrageous secret. How are we going to keep it a little secret?"

"Good question, Eddie," Borstrand said.

"May I answer that, Bobby?" Julie asked.

"Certainly."

Julie leaned forward on the couch and said, "Eddie, you've been a good and trusted friend of ours for many years. We love you as a family member. You are our daughter's godfather. We trust you with her life. We can't think of anyone who would do a better job of raising her. But we really need your help this time. I know you're the only one who can do this."

"Just what is 'this'?" Rowland asked.

"We need you, once you throw your hat into the ring, to systematically eliminate my competition one by one, until you're the last man standing. Then we will run against each other, and I will win."

Rowland had to smile at that. "You think it's that easy?"

"No," Julie said, "of course not. But to preserve our democracy, this is something that must be done."

"Why?"

"The United States has never had a female president, and I'm really not sure if the people are ready for one, but if you make yourself so obnoxious to our fellow Americans, they will be forced to vote for me."

"You sure about that?"

"I'm sure that you can plan it that way."

Rowland stood and walked to the dirty windows overlooking 23rd Street. He peered through the grime and clenched his teeth. He said,

"This place is disgusting. I never thought I would be caught dead in a place like this. But you've forced my hand." He turned around and looked at the Borstrands. "So, you think I can make myself so disgustingly ugly and obnoxious that you'll win easily."

"Something like that," Borstrand admitted.

Rowland shook his head and said, "I don't like it. This city hates me enough as it is. Why should I go out of my way to make the rest of the country hate me?"

"Because if you don't, you'll have a republican in the White House who will undo all the good work Charles has done."

"You think Charles"--referring to the current president— "has done that much good?"

"Yes," Borstrand said, "we do, and we have to keep on moving forward and not backwards. The world is changing, Eddie, and we have to change with it or die. The republicans want to keep the status quo. That will strangle our democracy and assure its death. Unless we do something about it."

"You guys are pretty sure about all of this."

"Yes, we are," Julie said. "From all the polls we've taken and everyone we've spoken to, we know that this country is ready for a change, just as the rest of the world is doing. We must act, or be lost."

"Stop with the melodramatics," Rowland scoffed. "You act as if our country is on the verge of total destruction."

"Well, if you don't see it," Borstrand said, "then we don't have anything more to talk about."

"Now wait a minute, wait a minute," Rowland said hastily, trying to be soothing, a part of him that he didn't show very often. "Hold your horses. I didn't say I wouldn't do it. I just need to think about it and discuss it with Carlotta."

"But you must not tell her what's behind it all," Julie cautioned.

"I can't even tell my wife?"

"No one must know but the three of us," Borstrand said

Rowland shook his head and asked, "How are we going to keep such a thing a secret?"

"We need to keep our mouths shut," Julie insisted. "Nobody—even your closest friends mustn't know."

"It's a big secret to keep," Rowland said.

"Yes, it is," Julie confirmed, "but doable."

"I have to think about it," Rowland said after a moment.

"You have until tomorrow morning," Julie said. "I'll give you that much time. But after that, it'll be too late. We need to get the ball rolling as soon as possible."

Rowland shook his head and said, "I understand. You'll get my answer first thing tomorrow morning."

"Sounds great," Julie said as she stood and held out her hand.

Rowland went over to her, and she leaned in for a kiss on the cheek. He reluctantly obliged.

Borstrand showed him to the door and shook his hand before he left. Borstrand returned to the living room and made himself another drink.

He looked at his wife. "What do you think?" he asked her.

She was sitting on the couch again. "He'll do it," she answered.

And she smiled.

2

Michael Espinoza was leaning back in his chair at The New York Herald Tribune, enjoying the silence when the phone broke it. He was a big man, at least 6'1", with a large barrel chest that sloped down to a well-manicured stomach. His legs were thick with muscle, and the pants were carefully wrapped around his sculpted lower body. His hair was jet black and slicked down, and his handsome, rugged face was hairless.

The phone rang a second time, loudly and shrilly, and he looked down at it with derision. He hated the phone. That's why he didn't use a cellphone very often, which his colleagues thought foolhardy, but it didn't stop him from scooping the others in the large newsroom. He finally rested his feet on the floor and reached for the receiver, when the third ring stopped him. What was he doing? He didn't want anymore news for the day. He wanted to relax and enjoy the quiet.

The phone rang a fourth time. His hand hesitated some more, and then he grabbed the phone from its hook and barked, "Yeah?"

"Mike?" asked a familiar voice. "Is that you?"

"What do you want, Pedro?" Mike asked, very tired.

Pedro was one of his CIs, and he always looked forward to talking to him. But not tonight. He was too exhausted to hunt down a lead. Tell him to call tomorrow, he thought. But then he wondered if the confidential information Pedro was about to give him was worth anything. He couldn't afford to pass it up.

"Listen," Pedro went on without hesitation, "I've got some incredible news..."

"It's always incredible with you," Michael said wearily.

"No, listen, this is really good."

"Okay, what is it?"

Pedro paused before saying, "Eddie Rowland's throwing his hat in the ring."

"For what?" Michael asked. "Garbage collector?"

"Very funny. What do you think Big Eddie would throw his hat in the ring for?"

Michael shrugged even though Pedro couldn't see him. "I have no idea," he said.

"Get this," Pedro said dramatically. "He's going to run for president."

There was silence while Michael digested this.

"Mike, you still there?"

Michael was stunned. He sat there with the phone about to drop from his hand. "Where'd you hear this?" he finally asked.

"I got my sources."

"I'm sure."

"No, really, Mike, this is pure gold."

"When's he going to announce?"

"I don't know that for sure, but I know it's gonna be soon."

"Not many details," Michael said skeptically.

"What do you want? An engraved invitation?"

"That would help."

"C'mon, Mike, be realistic."

There was an extended pause.

Finally, Michael asked, "How much?"

"A coupla C's," Pedro said promptly.

Michael laughed. "Are you insane? No way."

"Please, Mike," Pedro pleaded, "you gottta do this for me."

A silence followed.

Then, "Who's after you?" Michael asked.

Pedro hesitated before saying, "Connor Binghamton," quietly.

"The Big Con himself? How'd you get mixed up with the Irish mafia?"

"A long story."

"I got time."

"Well, I don't," Pedro insisted. "Please help me, Mike."

"Where?"

"Lucy's."

"When?"

"An hour, okay?"

"I'll be there," Michael said and hung up before Pedro could say "thank you."

***

Lucy's was a diner on Third Avenue. When Mike got there, Pedro was already seated in a booth at the back. He was a weaselly-looking man, short and thin with a narrow face, and a protruding nose. He wasn't very good-looking, and he knew it and used it to his advantage. Unfortunately, he had run out of options and obviously needed Mike's help.

Mike sidled up to the booth while Pedro was involved with his phone, and when Mike sat across from him, Pedro finally looked up.

"Thank God you're here," he said. "Do you have the money?"

"First," Mike said, "I need to know where you got the information from."

"Why's that so important?" Pedro asked.

"Because I need to know who your sources are."

"Does everybody know your sources?"

"Of course not."

"Then why do you need to know mine?"

"I want to see how reliable they are."

"Mike," Pedro said conspiratorially, "take it from me. This is gold."

"Boy," Mike said, shaking his head, "you're full of cliches tonight, aren't you?"

Pedro asked, "Where's the money?" impatiently.

Mike pulled an envelope from his inside coat pocket and tossed it on the table in front of Pedro who grabbed it greedily, opened it, and counted the money.

"What?" Mike said, "you don't trust me?"

"I don't trust nobody," Pedro snarled in his most weaselly voice.

'Please, no double negatives. I'm a writer, after all."

"What's it to you?"

"You're in one hell of a mood tonight."

"Well, wouldn't you be if the Big Con was breathing down your neck?"

"I wouldn't be in trouble with him in the first place."

Pedro counted the money a second time.

"You really don't trust me," Mike said wonderingly.

"It's not that, Mike, it's just that I'm so nervous I can't stop what I'm doing. I have to get over there and hand this in."

He started to get up. Mike held him by the arm.

"Not so fast," he said. "I need to know who your source is."

"Oh, come on, Mike," Pedro said, trying to pull away, "give me a break, will you?"

"Only if you tell me who your source is," Mike insisted.

"I can't tell you…"

"Yes, you can. If you don't," Mike warned, "the money-well might just dry up."

"Even is the info is good?"

"Even then."

Pedro dropped back into his seat and looked around them conspiratorially. "Okay," he said in a whisper, "but you can't tell anybody else."

"Cross my heart," Mike said as he actually crossed his heart, but with the fingers of his other hand behind his back crossed as well.

Pedro looked around again. Then he said, "It's Brad Cummings."

"Rowland's personal assistant?"

"That's right."

"But why should he want to make it tough for his boss?"

"Because he hates him like rat poison."

Mike leaned back in his seat. "Really?"

"You swore you wouldn't tell anybody else."

"I did."

"Did you have your fingers crossed?" Pedro asked suspiciously.

Mike smiled at him. "Now would I do that?" he asked, as he crossed his fingers again under the table.

"Good," Pedro said, trusting him. "Now I really gotta go."

"Be my guest," Mike said, gesturing with his arm.

"See ya," Pedro said, and he scooted out of the diner.

Mike asked for a cup of coffee, and as he sat there sipping it, he thought of all the harm Rowland could do. He certainly had the money to buy his way into the White House, but once there, he could destroy democracy at its core. But why should he want to do that? As far as Mike knew, Rowland had always been a Democrat. Now, he was going to run as a republican. There was only one reason for that: he wanted to become an autocrat, a dictator. Now wait a minute, he told himself, your imagination is running away with itself. Do you really think Rowland is enough of a rat to do such a thing? He would never underestimate the man. This is something that needed to be looked into. Rowland ran his real estate empire like he was a Mafia don. Why not run the country the same way? That's ridiculous, Mike thought. He wouldn't have the nerve. After all, Mike had always thought of him as an imbecile, someone who would take money from his father, and when that ran out, because he would run a business into the ground, he would take some more and then some more and then... He had always said that the country should be run like a business. That's because he wasn't a politician and didn't know what he was talking about. But he could give it a try, Mike knew that. Rowland could run the country into the ground the same way he ran all of his businesses. It was a scary thought.

3

It was 9:30 p.m. when Rowland entered his suite of rooms. They were on the top floor of Rowland Enterprises. They took up the whole floor. Rowland liked it that way. He enjoyed his privacy, especially from those he considered commoners and not worth associating with. He placed his keys in the silver bowl, which rested on the ornate sideboard just inside the front door. He walked across the marble floor until he got to the living room, where he sat on the plush sofa in the center of the room. He stared into the unlit fireplace. It wasn't cold enough for a fire, he thought. His mind was alive with thoughts at that moment. He was still confused by the meeting he had just had. He just couldn't understand why the Borstrands wanted his help to clinch the presidency. Julie was practically a shoe-in. But then again, he knew that on the republican side, Bud Congreve was part of a dynasty. After all, his older brother Arnold had already served as president, and his father had served as vice president under Andrew Reynolds and then served one term as president himself. The republicans loved the Congreves; they were still practically the first family of the United States.

He heard the soft swish of satin as his wife, Carlotta, entered the room. She came from the Eastern part of Europe, but her first name was given to her by her mother who was Spanish, while her father was of Romanian descent. She was tall and lovely, at least thirty years younger than Rowland, with an Eastern European cast to her face that had made her extremely popular when she had been a model. She approached the well-stocked wet bar in the corner and poured herself a sherry, which she sipped luxuriously. She looked at Rowland with disdain while she drank and leaned forward, resting her elbows on the glass surface of the bar. She drank some more sherry. She knew

Rowland didn't like her drinking, and she didn't care. If Rowland hadn't been rich, she would have left him long ago. Their only child, Ronald, was not his anyway. She'd had an affair with a beautiful man some ten years ago and become pregnant by him because she didn't want to bring another Rowland into the world, another Rowland who could help to destroy the fabric of American society, which she cherished so much. She loathed Rowland, and she was sure he knew it. He had cheated on her time and time again, and not even with respectable women but with prostitutes and porno stars. He was a disgusting person, and there were many in New York who felt the same.

Carlotta began the conversation in her heavy Slavic accent. "So? What was that all about?" In private, her English was immaculate, while in public she reverted to her pidgin English in order to fool strangers.

Rowland came out of his trance and turned to her. He made a face when he saw the sherry in her hand. "What was what all about?" he asked.

"Your meeting. What did the Borstrands want?"

"Oh, nothing," he said flippantly. "Just a meeting between old friends."

"Yeah, sure. You know I don't believe that for a minute."

"It doesn't matter what you think."

"I know that's how you feel," she purred sexily, "but no matter what, I'm still your wife."

He thought for a moment, then said, "Okay. How would you like to be First Lady of the United States?"

She almost choked on her drink. "What?" she sputtered. "Are you out of your mind?"

He smiled. "I just might be," he confirmed.

"You mean," she said slowly, "you're going to be president?"

"I just might be. I have to run first, you know, and be elected."

"Do you think that's possible?"

"I don't know," Rowland said as he stroked his chin. "It just might happen."

"What are you thinking, Eddie?"

"We'll see."

"What will we see?"

"What might happen in the future."

She poured another sherry. "I really do think you've gone crazy," she said as she twirled her index finger in her drink, then inserted her index finger in her mouth and erotically sucked on it because she knew it drove her husband crazy with desire.

"You do, huh?"

"You're not a politician. You've never held any office at all."

"Anybody can run for president. It's in the constitution. It just takes a lot of money."

"Which you have."

"That's right."

Now, the entire world will know what a despicable human being he is, she thought. He doesn't have enough self-control to contain his baser instincts. He is a pig.

"Why must you always drag me into one of your schemes?" she asked in an exasperated manner.

"You think this is a scheme?" he demanded.

"Well, isn't it? You're full of schemes, aren't you? Most of them are illegal. You've just been very lucky not to have been convicted.

Otherwise, you'd be spending the rest of your life behind bars."

He snickered and said, "You think you're so smart. That's how much you know about me."

"I know enough about you to damage your reputation."

There was a silence as he scanned her with his evil eyes. "So beautiful," he said, "and yet so dangerous."

"I have learned some things from you."

"Yes, you have," he admitted. "But not enough to destroy me before I kick you out on the street with that pretty bastard son of yours."

She paused before saying, "How long have you known?"

"Shit, you must think I'm really stupid. You think I was gonna trust you? I had you follow from the very beginning. I knew you were pregnant before you did."

"You fucking son-of-a-bitch," she snarled, and then she spit at him. Unfortunately, he wasn't close enough to her to get any spittle on his face.

"You're a gorgeous woman, and the only reason you'd marry someone like me is for my money."

"If you think that, then why did you marry me in the first place?"

"Because you looked so good on my arm when we went out together. You're a nice piece of eye-candy, and I appreciate that. You know, from the very beginning, we've led separate lives. You go your way and I go mine. When we're seen together, it's for some reason or another. You don't like me. I know that. I'm not that crazy about you, but I'm still turned on when I get the chance to see you naked. I still get a hard-on and usually I have to jerk off to relieve myself or go see some high-class hooker, where I know I won't get some disease."

"You're disgusting."

"You're right," Rowland agreed, "but you're just as disgusting as I am." She gave him the evil eye, and he smiled mischievously. "Now," he continued, "how would you like to be First Lady of the United States?"

She shook her head. "This is not what I signed up for," she stated calmly.

"No, maybe not, but no matter what, you're along for the ride. Get it?"

She slowly returned to the wet bar to pour another sherry. She took a sip of it before saying, "What would I have to do?"

"A little research first."

"You want me to do homework?" she asked, horrified.

"Yes, but it's pretty painless. First, start watching CNN or MSNBC. Anything that involves the First Lady. Observe what she does, how she acts, especially with the president, how she responds to questions when or if she's asked any. All you would have to do is stay in the background, looking gorgeous. Do you think you can do that?"

The ends of her mouth curved into something like a smile. "I think I can do that," she said, not at all modestly.

"Good. Then your homework starts now." He grabbed the remote control of the 75" television hanging on the wall. He turned it to CNN. "Be observant, like a little kid."

"Then what happens?"

"We'll see about that. First, I have to get the nomination."

"Do you think you can do it?"

"I don't know. I have a plan, though. Only time will tell."

4

Julie Borstrand hung up the phone, making sure her carefully lacquered nails did not chip; they cost a good deal of money. She and her husband were still at the hotel in Chelsea; she had been talking on the landline there because she had asked Rowland to call her there; consequently, no one could track her phone calls.

She took a sip of her martini and said to her husband, "He's in."

Borstrand laughed jovially and clapped his hands with glee. "Early answer, but just as secure. Hello, White House, here we come again."

"You're pretty confident about my victory."

"Why shouldn't I be? After all, when I was president, they loved me."

She nodded and said, "So they did. In spite of your indiscretions."

"Leave me alone about that. When are you going to stop bringing up that old subject?"

"When we're both rotting in our graves."

He shook his head from side to side. "You sure know how to put a damper on a party."

"Yes, that's me," she confirmed. "Ms. Wet Blanket."

Borstrand went to the bar and fixed himself another drink.

Julie followed and stood across from him as he poured the alcohol. "If it weren't for me, you jackass, you wouldn't even have been president."

"Oh, yeah," Rowland sputtered.

"Oh, that's very mature."

"How about Ray?"

"How about him?"

"Wouldn't you say he was the architect of my campaign?"

"Yes, he was, but he acted on my orders."

"As always," he said, walking away, "you always have to be in control. From the very beginning of our relationship."

They had met in law school and immediately started seeing each other. Julie was a naïve, uninformed young lady, while Borstrand was a cockshound. He plowed his way through the young ladies at the school with a determination that amazed his friends, and even his enemies. When told of Borstrand's prowess with the ladies, Julie became intrigued. She wondered why he would be interested in a plain Jane with no money and no particular future. Eventually, Borstrand received a Rhodes Scholarship from Oxford and moved posthaste to England, where he spent the next two years fulfilling a dream. When he returned to the States, he searched for Julie, and when he found her, he asked her to marry him. She was in the middle of a rather cool relationship with a fellow student, so it was no bother to break it off. Neither one of them seemed particularly anguished about it. She immediately ran to a Justice of the Peace with Borstrand by her side, and they were married in a small, very private ceremony. It wasn't long after the ceremony that Julie discovered Borstrand was cheating on her; he couldn't seem to keep his cock where it belonged. Instead of divorcing Borstrand, she remained by his side because she had great hopes for him and wanted to be the First Lady of the United States, and then possibly move on to the presidency herself, a dream that she had held ever since she was a precocious child and her mother told her that she was destined for greatness. But she laid down the law with Borstrand.

"Listen, Bobby," she had informed him, "I was aware you were a cockshound when I met you, and I was aware of it when we married. But if you intend to continue your extracurricular activities, please try to be discreet. Otherwise, I will cut off your balls and feed them to you."

"That's being rather blunt."

"Do you agree to it?"

"You have my word," he had said.

"As far as I'm concerned, that doesn't mean much."

In spite of his indiscretions, Julie and Borstrand continued to have sex together until they conceived their daughter, Andrea, who was born on Christmas Day; Julie called Andrea her Immaculate Conception. Then, the sex stopped between them, and so Borstrand, in his mind, had a reason for fooling around. Only this time it increased in volume tenfold, and when he became president, he had a sexual relationship with one of his interns, which he vehemently denied in front of Congress, which led to his impeachment in the House, but was overturned in the Senate. Borstrands' democratic buddies came through for him.

This is why there was a definite feeling of contempt between them. They only remained together because it was difficult enough for a woman to run for president, but a divorced woman would make it impossible. So, they tolerated each other for the sake of her career. Someday she might live to regret it, but she had to admit that she had grown fond of him, in her way. He was like an old shaggy dog that she had gotten used to. She would pet him occasionally, and then he would retreat to his corner, where he would stay until he was needed again. And needed he would be, because when he left the presidency, he pulled in more of the popular vote than any of his predecessors. He was still very popular, and he knew it.

"Can we finally get out of this dump?" he asked his wife now.

"Why? You don't like it here? I thought you'd feel at home."

Borstrand gave her a look that would have killed if Julie had cared. But she didn't care anymore. She was her own woman, and didn't need him except for his speeches, which always wowed the spectators. When it came to politics, he reigned supreme.

"Well, you can stay here if you want," Borstrand said. "I'm getting the hell out."

"Be my guest. Just remember to put your disguise on before leaving."

"I will," he said as he wrapped the scarf around his face and placed the Stetson on his head to cover the mane of white hair. He stepped to the door quickly and just as quickly went out, leaving Julie alone, which is the way she liked it.

The former First Lady was pleased with herself. She sat on the decrepit sofa with a smug smile on her handsome face and thought about what she had already accomplished so far. She now had Rowland on a short leash, and she would have to keep him there. But he could be headstrong, and she had to watch out for that. She was headstrong herself, as her husband liked to say continuously, and she needed to watch it sometimes because it could make her rude and unlikable. If she didn't watch herself, she could lose a lot of votes from Midwesterners who didn't like easterners of any fashion; they were snobs just as much as the elite were, only in the reverse. She had to be careful when talking to them because she could turn them off with just the wrong expression. She had to show happiness at all times; they liked that. She got up from the sofa and wandered into the bedroom where she lay on the bed, not afraid of bedbugs in the least; after all, she'd had the suite fumigated before taking up temporary residence there, without telling Borstrand anything about it. The less he knows, the better, she thought, laughing to herself. He's such a dolt sometimes. What did I ever see in him in the first place? What a mistake it had been. But he was the father of Andrea, so she had to show him some respect and affection even though he didn't deserve it. If it weren't for him, however, she wouldn't be in the position she was in right now. She owed him that much, she knew. He may be a horse's ass, she told herself, but he did have his uses.

5

When Borstrand reached the street, he stood there trying very hard to calm down. Julie could really get to him, and she knew it, too; that's why she could be so infuriatingly mean at times. He breathed in the cool, fresh air and exhaled with a vengeance.

Fortunately, he did not attract a crowd because of his disguise, but he didn't stick around to make sure of it. He walked briskly to 8th Avenue, where he quickly picked up a cab and gave the driver an address in midtown near Times Square.

It was a run-down looking hotel on 49th Street. But looks can be deceiving, of course, for the interior was a plush red velvet where Borstrand was greeted by a young, half-dressed female who welcomed him graciously; she knew who he was: he had been there many times before. It was the most popular bordello in Manhattan, exclusively attended by those in the know with plenty of money in their pockets. Powerful men who had gotten bored with their marriages, the same old sexual routine that they had been practicing from the very beginning. Either that, or their wives were cheating on them with much younger men who were looking to become powerful themselves but didn't have the means to do so. So, they manipulated the powerful women they fucked into thinking they had the mental capacity to build a life behind the scenes where they could manipulate the little people into thinking they were important.

Borstrand chose a full-figured Hispanic young lady whom he had fucked before. She led him by the hand to her room, where she undressed, and then proceeded to undress him, and while she was on her knees, she sucked his cock for a little while until he grew tired of that. Then he brought her to her feet, turned her around, bent her over the bed, and proceeded to go through the motions of fucking her from behind. But his thoughts were somewhere else: he couldn't stop thinking of his arrogant wife, someone he had truly loved once and still loved in his heart. But unfortunately, she was a person who didn't know how to love back. She put on a good show, but she was cold-hearted and only interested in one thing: her own ambitions.

When Borstrand first met her, he was a brilliant law student and she was a petite young thing, with aspirations that rivalled his. He wanted to get into her pants the moment he saw her, even though she was not the best-looking piece of tail on the campus. But she was extremely bright and a great debater. In fact, Borstrand had debated her on more than one occasion; in his opinion, she had beaten him all three times, but in a male-dominated society such as the one they inhabited at the time, he came out the winner. They went to bed shortly after the first debate; she was unskilled but willing to learn; she was an apt pupil. They rutted like animals every chance they could. Then he disappeared, leaving Julie stranded with her emotions left out in the open; she didn't know how to react. She cried for days on end. She didn't think she'd ever recover.

Meanwhile, Borstrand had taken his Rhodes Scholarship to Oxford without saying a word to anyone. But while in England, he couldn't get Julie out of his mind, even though he had his pick of many of the British female students who were his classmates. He thought about her regularly and even masturbated at times when she inhabited his mind. Two years later, he returned and sought her out. He remembered the moment when they saw each other again; the look of astonishment in her eyes was enough to give him an erection. He asked her to marry him on the spot, and she accepted without hesitation.

They were married the next week, and the first years were blissful. But, as was to be expected, Borstrand got bored and started on his extracurricular activities without thinking twice about it. Julie found out about his first affair because he wasn't very discreet about it. She was very hurt and went on a jealous tirade, thinking she had put him in his place. He acted abashed and told her over and over how sorry he was and promised never to do it again. She forgave him reluctantly, knowing that his word meant nothing. Very soon after this, Borstrand cheated again, but he was more discreet this time. They remained married because they both had the same dream: to occupy the White House.

However, Julie's dream was a great deal more realistic than his. After their first and only child was born, Julie lost interest in sex. All she could think of was working for her husband to be president. It took quite a few years, but she finally dusted him off, made him presentable, and revealed him to the American public. He looked to be a down-to-earth, humble Southern boy; he looked like someone they could trust. They voted him in by a landslide, throwing out the complacent incumbent—the elder Congreve--who hadn't done anything for the people, only the very rich. And when her husband was reelected, her hopes rose even higher, in spite of the scandal between Borstrand and an intern who performed fellatio on him. Despite this outrageous scandal, Borstrand left the White House with a higher popularity rating than any other president before him. His wife's aspirations soared even higher.

Now he was there in that room of a whorehouse, pounding a Hispanic whore from behind. He could feel his balls fill with sperm and his cock grow harder. He made a loud squeaking noise when he came inside her. His spent cock slid out of the whore's pussy, but he felt drained, not by excitement but by the lack of it. When he came, he felt the excitement of coming in the intern's mouth, but coming inside the whore's pussy left him feeling alienated. By the time all these thoughts had drifted through his mind, the whore had cleaned herself up thoroughly and put her clothes back on. Borstrand stood there naked, his limp cock hanging loosely between his white, unattractive legs.

The whore smiled at him, kissed him on the cheek, and left the room with a flirtatious smack on his ass. His cock did not respond. He got dressed glumly, making sure he put on his disguise, and left the establishment without looking at anyone standing in the hallway or out on the street. A cab was passing as his feet hit the sidewalk; he raised his hand; the cab stopped for him; he climbed in and gave the driver his home address on Fifth Avenue. He was through for the night.

6

Litzy Baker was working on Eddie Rowland while he lay naked on the bed, his huge belly blocking his view of what she was doing to his cock. Not that it made any difference: his cock was completely unresponsive. It lay there flaccid and ugly as sin. Litzy had never been sexually attracted to Rowland, but he paid her enough money to make it all right for her to work on him whenever he wanted.

So, she was working on him right then, between his legs, bent over, his cock in her mouth. He wasn't even moaning with pleasure. He was staring at the ceiling, his eyes glued to the moving fan, his mouth twisted in a cruel face.

Litzy continued her actions, until it was obvious that nothing was going to happen: his cock remained a flaccid junk heap. She sat up on her haunches, her beautiful breasts displayed for him to see. But instead, his eyes darted back and forth as the fan moved in captivating ways. Finally, he realized that she was no longer sucking him, and he looked at her. The cruelness of his expression usually frightened her, but not tonight. He no longer intimidated her. She thought of him as a buffoon. He was big and ugly and horribly formed, his breasts drooping over his large belly, which was hard as a rock. Litzy thought he must have something wrong with his gut: it wasn't soft and squishy, the way large bellies were supposed to be; it was solid as a boulder, a mountain of distorted flesh; the only workout Rowland got was when he walked from his building to his chauffeured limousine. What an asshole he is, she thought.

"What's the matter?" Rowland asked. "Why'd you stop?"

"You don't seem much into it," Litzy commented as she flipped his cock around nonchalantly.

He couldn't see over his belly, so he raised his head and noticed his inactive cock. "Yeah, I guess you're right." He laid his head back and continued to stare at the whirling fan.

"You have something on your mind?" she asked.

"What would you think if I ran for president?"

She didn't answer right away because she knew that if her answer was one he didn't like, her revenue might dry up. He was a mean bastard, not caring one way or the other if someone didn't have enough money to live on.

She smiled and said, "Are you thinking about it?" as a delaying tactic.

"It has crossed my mind."

"Then go for it," she said enthusiastically.

He sat up and looked closely at her. "You really think so?"

"You got the money. Why the hell not?"

He nodded, then after a moment he asked, "Would you vote for me?"

There it is, she thought, the million-dollar question. How should she answer it? In the affirmative, of course, although she would never vote for the scum. "Of course I'd vote for you," she said, leaning forward to take his cock back into her mouth.

The fact that she had complimented him on his possible decision made him excited, and his cock grew in her mouth until it was an actual hard-on. She sucked and sucked and massaged his balls until he came in her mouth with a groan. She sucked him dry, then went into the bathroom of the hotel suite that he had rented for the night. A lot better than that other piece of shit he was in earlier that night, he thought.

Litzy closed the bathroom door behind her and used the complimentary mouthwash to take the taste of him out of her mouth. He tasted awful, but she knew he liked to come in her mouth, so she allowed it, even though his sperm rested uncomfortably in the pit of her stomach. In fact, she felt like throwing it up, but she knew he'd get mad at her, so she kept it down and eventually shit it out. When she was done in the bathroom, she opened the door with a big smile on her face and posed in the doorway, her naked body teasing him.

He was sitting up with his back against the headboard. "You look beautiful," he said admiringly.

"Thank you. Do you feel better now?"

He chuckled. "Much." He was unconscious of his nakedness and, in some way, portrayed it boldly, in spite of the fact that it was a very disgusting scene.

At least that's what Litzy thought, but she would never tell him that, of course. He was an egomaniacal fool, and he thought he was a gift to women from god himself. She knew, however, that he did not believe in any higher spiritual power. As a matter of fact, he felt he was more powerful than any god, if such a being existed. His wife didn't serve him, if she ever did, that is. Litzy suspected that their son did not bear his genes, even though he bore his name. No, Rowland had three grown children by his first marriage, and they were creepy as is. Children of the corn, she thought, although she knew someone else had said it first, but whom she could not remember. Maybe it was Saturday Night Live. It suddenly dawned on her that she hadn't watched SNL in a long time and that she should because it always proved to be a hoot.

But now she was faced with his limp dick and massive belly. He displayed them both with pride. She wished she could tell him how she felt, but she knew he would ruin her if she did. Instead, she sidled up to him and started kissing him from the top of his toes to the top of his head; she wanted a tip from him, perhaps even an enormous tip. She straddled and rubbed her pussy against his dick until he started to get hard again. She wrapped her arms around him and kissed his thick, disgusting lips. She took his hardness and slipped him inside her. She rode him until he squirted inside her and lay back with a relaxed smile on his ugly face.

Satisfied, he said, "That was great."

She smiled up at him but didn't say anything because she didn't want the way she felt to be reflected in her voice. Instead, she laid cozily with him, her head on his chest, and the index finger of her left hand playing with his nipple. He liked that, and his cock began to come alive again. Oh, my God, she thought, he must have taken Viagra. She instantly stopped arousing him with her finger, sat up, and swung her legs over the side of the bed.

"How was it for you?" he asked smugly.

The age-old question, she thought, was usually asked by men who were selfish in the bedroom. "Just fantastic," she squealed in a very upbeat voice.

Rowland chuckled, and it was at this point that Litzy slid off the bed and entered the bathroom again, where she washed up and made sure that the stink of him did not remain on her skin.

Then she hurriedly got dressed, went back into the bedroom, and said, "Gotta go, baby, I'm late for another appointment." There was no other appointment, but she couldn't stick around him much longer or she'd literally throw up. She stood her ground, though, and waited for him to reach for his wallet, which he did and pulled out five one-thousand-dollar bills. She grabbed them hastily and made for the door to the suite, her delicious ass twitching him a goodbye.

He smiled some more, and after the door closed behind her, he fell into a deep, troubled sleep. Why troubled? he thought when he finally woke up. What do I have to be troubled about? He couldn't remember the dreams he had just had; they vanished into the air once he awakened. Before he became fully awake, however, he reached out to grab something or someone that was facing him, but it broke apart and fell into a million pieces at his feet. Then the pieces grew tentacles and wrapped themselves around his legs, up around his torso, until they were wrapped around his throat, strangling him. When he couldn't breathe, he woke up. It was his damn sleep apnea, and he didn't have his oxygen machine.

He got out of bed and went into the bathroom, and stared at himself in the mirror; he flexed his nonexistent muscles. I still have it, he thought, and while still looking at himself in the mirror, he thought, Not bad for a man my age. He looked down at himself and tried to see his cock from that angle, but his belly obscured the view. He tried sucking it in, but it was no good. All he needed, he thought, was a little exercise, and it would be gone in no time. He was used to telling himself things that weren't true. He turned on the shower and stepped into it when the temperature was to his liking. He wanted to get the stink of sex off him so he wouldn't have to hear Carlotta complain. If there was one thing she could sense, it was when he'd had sex; it was like some kind of extrasensory perception with her. He scrubbed himself down, especially his genitals, not that Carlotta ever got close to them; she hadn't been near them since they were first married, and she only went near them that night because she was drunk on Dom Perignon and didn't realize who she was having sex with. In the morning, she saw him lying next to her, and she ran into the bathroom and puked into the toilet. It was a disgusting sound coming from such a beautiful woman, and he never forgot it. But she was still his trophy wife and looked good on his arm at all-important functions. He could afford her, and that was all that mattered.

He stepped out of the shower and toweled himself off, then returned to the bedroom of the luxurious suite to catch some sleep. But before doing that, he called housekeeping to come up to his room and remake the bed. When the young, pretty maid was through, he patted her on the butt, which she didn't like one bit, slipped her some money, and after she was gone, he made himself comfortable and turned on the flatscreen TV on the wall across from him to a porno channel. Eventually he knew he would get hard again, and he'd masturbate to the lovely women who were performing for his pleasure. Ah, it was a great life, he thought. The city would disagree with him.

7

Mike Espinosa was roaming the streets at 3:20 in the morning. He was restless, and he didn't know what to do with himself. So he stopped in a bar on Third Avenue and had a rum and Coke, which he practically inhaled. He ordered a second one, then a third one, which he nursed until after four. Then he continued south on Third, his thoughts swirling around inside his head. He couldn't understand why he couldn't sit still, and he especially couldn't understand why he couldn't sleep.

His thoughts constantly returned to Eddie Rowland. Was the man really enough of a blowhard to think he could become president? Well, as P. T. Barnum put it, no one ever went broke underestimating the public. As he wandered, his cell phone vibrated in his pocket. He took it out and answered it.

It was the night manager at the paper. Andy Ransom. Strict sort of guy. "Listen, Eddie Rowland is holding a press conference at his place tomorrow at noon. Be there."

Mike was wary. "What's it about?" he asked defensively.

"Go there and find out," Ransom said and disconnected.

Well, Mike thought, I guess Pedro was right: Rowland is going to make the announcement official. So he continued on his way to a rat-hole in the East Village known as The Mole, an appropriate name for a mole to hang out in. The darkness of the bar was disconcerting at first, but Mike got used to it and looked around for Pedro. No sign of him. He went up to the bar.

"Seen Pedro lately?" Mike asked the bartender.

The bartender said, "He was here about an hour ago."

"Know where he went?"

The bartender shook his head. "He'll be back," he said.

"In that case," Mike said, "I'll have a beer."

As he nursed his beer, he looked around at what he considered the dregs of humanity: human scum living in the darkness, crawling around on all fours and looking to make a buck in any dishonest way they knew how. These were animals who did not like working for a living, so they kept their ears wide open in case some information leaked into them that they could then inform on. They were ugly-looking, rat-like forms who scurried around making a living by making others' lives miserable. They got some kind of satisfaction from destroying people's lives.

Mike finished his beer, and before he could ask for another one, the door opened and a cop walked in. He could tell it was a cop because of the way he handled himself. He was tall and thin and plain in the face. He was the sort of nondescript personality that you'd forget the instant after meeting him.

The cop walked up to the bartender. "You got a guy here by the name of David Lopez?" he asked.

"Who wants to know?" the bartender responded.

The cop pulled out his badge and flashed it. The bartender hooked a finger toward a door in the rear. The cop headed that way and disappeared through the door.

Mike turned to the bartender. "Who's David Lopez?"

"None of your business."

Mike smiled. "Thanks for the information."

After a moment, the cop reappeared and walked out into the street.

Mike looked after him, then back at the bartender, who had

retreated to help some other customers. So Mike got off his stool and walked to the door in the back and knocked. There was a muffled "Come in," and he stepped through the door. The room was just as dim and uncluttered as the bar. There was only one occupant, who Mike supposed was David Lopez, a man in his late forties with a creased face and brown complexion who must have weighed at least 300 pounds.

"Mr. Lopez?" Mike asked.

"Who the fuck are you?"

"Someone curious."

"Huh?" Lopez was as dumb as he looked.

Mike stepped further into the room. "I'm a reporter for the Herald-Tribune."

"Who the fuck let you in here?"

"It's a bar. No one let me in."

Lopez smirked and said, "I don't talk to reporters."

"That's too bad," Mike said. "I need a story."

"And I need you to get the fuck out of here."

"I can't until you tell me what the cop was doing here."

"What the fuck's that your business?"

"I'm always interested in what cops are doing."

"Then why don't you go ask him?" Lopez growled.

"Because I think you might be more conducive to talking."

"Conducive, huh?" Lopez grunted. "I like that. I've never heard it used in a conversation."

Maybe he isn't as dumb as he appears to be, Mike thought. I'll have to rethink my assessment.

Mike said, "Then can we talk?"

Lopez gestured to a chair across from him. "Sit," he said.

Mike sat and crossed his legs to make himself more comfortable. "So what was the cop doing here?"

Lopez scoffed, "Oh, that. Just delivering some news about an employee of mine."

"Anybody I know?"

"You might. Pedro Armendariz."

"What about him?"

"He's dead."

"Where?"

"Avenue C and 10th Street."

Mike looked down at the grimy floor. "That's too bad," he mumbled.

"You knew him?"

"Yes."

"You like him?"

"No."

"You gonna grieve about him?"

"No."

"Then get the fuck out of my office. We've talked enough."

Mike stood and turned, and walked to the door. "Can I ask one more question?"

"Make it fast."

"You know about Eddie Rowland?"

"What about him?"

"He's going to run for president."

"No shit," Lopez said in amazement as he sat back in his chair.

"He's going to announce it today."

"Well, I'll have to call him up and congratulate him."

Mike opened the door and went out. He walked numbly toward the door to the street and when he got there, he opened it and walked out. The street in front of him was empty because all the activity was at Avenue C and 10th Street. The lights of the police cars were flashing through the darkness, and a large crowd had gathered. Mike moved in that direction.

When he got there, he stood and stared. He could see over the heads of most of the crowd and saw something covered with a white sheet lying on the sidewalk. The sheet was streaked with blood from the body underneath. That used to be Pedro, he thought. I just saw him a few hours ago, and now he's lying there dead. I gave him the money to pay off his gambling debt, and now he's dead. How could this have happened?

All of a sudden, he heard his name being called from the perimeter of the scene. He looked over and saw that it was Herb Rinaldi, a detective from the 49th Precinct, gesturing for him to come over. So he turned and walked to where Herb stood, his hands on his hips, standing behind the crime scene tape.

"How'd you get here so soon?" Herb asked.

"I was in the area."

"Lucky you." Herb shrugged. "Well, it's a cut-and-dried suicide. Guy took a swan dive off that building." He pointed at a dingy brownstone across the street. "Landed headfirst. What a mess. The head split open like a watermelon. The only way we were able to identify him was by the ID in his wallet." He consulted his notes. "Name of Pedro Armendariz. From Queens."

Mike looked at him. "Then what was he doing down here?"

"Got no idea. What were you doing down here?"

"Taking a walk."

Herb was a man in his fifties, heavyset and of medium height. "At this time of the morning? You live way uptown."

"Is there a law against taking a walk?" Mike snapped.

"No," Herb acknowledged, "but it is kinda suspicious."

"Am I suspect?"

"Did you know the guy?"

Mike thought about that for a nanosecond. Then he said, "No," wondering why he was lying. He didn't owe Pedro anything, he guessed. Pedro was a member of the dregs of society, so no one would miss him.

"How do you know?" Herb asked suddenly.

Mike came to in a sudden. "Know what?"

"If you knew the guy."

"I don't know anybody this far downtown."

"What?" Herb said. "All your CIs live on the Upper East Side?"

'I don't have any Confidential Informants."

"Tell me another one."

Mike had to smile at that. Herb knew better than to believe such a thing. All reporters had CIs, and Mike was one of the best.

"So what are you doing down here?" Herb asked.

"I told you," Mike said. "I was taking a walk. I couldn't sleep."

"Okay, okay, but stick around for a while. I may need a statement from you."

"I have nothing to say."

"Yeah, sure," Herb said and walked away in the direction of the body.

Mike took the opportunity to walk away himself, moving swiftly across 10th Street to 4th Avenue until he reached the 14th Street IRT going uptown. He waited on the platform for less than ten minutes. The train was practically empty. Mike moved to the rear car. He sat down and instantly smelled a familiar scent.

Someone was smoking pot. He looked down the aisle and saw a young guy, long and lanky, with greasy long hair, smoking a joint. Suddenly, the door to the car opened, and a transit cop walked in. He stood there for a moment getting acclimated to the smell. Mike thought, Uh-oh, the guys going to get busted. But instead, the cop stood at one of the platform doors, holding on to a rail, and waited for the train to stop, which happened momentarily. When the doors opened, the cop walked out and down the platform, away from the hippie who could have caused him a lot of paperwork if he'd let him. But life was too short, Mike thought. Besides, in that day and age, the guy would have gotten nothing more than a slap on the wrist. Was it worth it? The cop obviously didn't think so.

When he got to his newspaper office, he sat at his desk and wrote up what he'd seen that night, including the transit cop's actions. Then he looked it over and sent it to the night editor's desk. The night editor approved it for the bottom of the front page, and Mike smiled. Then he put his chair back and went to sleep.

8

itzy Baker was working on her last customer of the night, Earl Lester, when he died of a massive heart attack. His penis remained erect as he quickly expired. She didn't know what to do at first, but then she realized she had to get out of there. She first wondered if she would be able to jerk him off to completion, but she wasn't into necrophilia, and she knew that that might not work. She didn't have the time for it anyway.

She went into the hotel bathroom and got a wet rag. She returned to the body and proceeded to wipe his dick off so she wouldn't leave any telltale traces of her DNA. She proceeded to wipe down the rest of the room, stripped the bed leaving the corpse without sheets, stuffed them into her carryall, went back into the bathroom where she took a hot shower, made sure everything of hers went down the drain, then returned to the bedroom where she got dressed, slung her carryall over her shoulder and left the room, then the hotel itself without causing any undue attention.

When she hit the street, she turned west and strode with her long, infinitely luscious legs to an after-hours bar she usually went to after work. It was crowded, but she found a space at the bar and sat on the stool. She knew the bartender, Joaquin, and ordered a whiskey and soda. He returned with it in a moment and leaned forward, his muscular arms resting on the bar.

"What's up, girl?" he asked. "You look kinda flushed."

"It's nothing," she said hurriedly, and took a large gulp of her drink.

"Liar," Joaquin said.

"Go away, Joaquin," Litzy said. "I have some thinking to do."

Joaquin stood up with his hands in a position of surrender and said, "Okay, girl, don't bite my head off. Take as much time as you need," and he moved away to the end of the bar.

Litzy sat there, nursing her drink, wondering what she was going to do. After all, she might have left something of herself behind that would lead to her identity. She had been booked twice for prostitution, and her fingerprints were on file. She thought back to her time after the death and to the hasty clean-up. She probably missed something, but the death wouldn't be discovered until later on that morning. A naked corpse lying there with his dick pointing to the sky. What a way to go, she thought. He was probably smiling all the way to the Pearly Gates; that is, if he deserved to go there.

In spite of her profession, Litzy was extremely religious. She was Catholic and believed in all that rigmarole. She laughed to herself. What would the nuns think of me now? she asked of herself. In their minds, I was already condemned to perdition. She chuckled some more. She'd been a bad girl in school and had caused many of the nuns' conniption fits, and now she was a bad adult girl. She would love to go to the school for a reunion dressed to the nines in her best slutty outfit and watch their faces as their jaws dropped to the ground and they started praying for her. What a riot that would be.

Then a thought popped into her head: What about Eddie Rowland? He had many connections who could help her out. They could dispose of the body and clean up afterwards. What a great idea, she thought. She looked at the time on her phone and saw that it was almost 4:30. Well, she knew that Eddie was a light sleeper and usually stayed up late. So she called his number and waited as it rang five times. Finally, Rowland answered, and she told him the whole story in one breathless gulp. He calmed her down with assurances that he would take care of everything, but she owed him one. Litzy agreed and broke the connection; she didn't want to talk to Rowland any longer than she had to. As she sat there, she began to cool down because she knew that Rowland would take care of the situation in his own way.

Fortunately, the noise of the bar drowned out anything she'd said over the phone. She was safe, she thought. She just had to keep her mouth shut. But there was one thing she wasn't sure of: Eddie Rowland, himself. Eddie was a hustler and a con artist; he was a thug in fancy clothes, even though the clothes he wore hung poorly on him. Perhaps he should get a new tailor; that is, if he had one and didn't buy off the rack. She wouldn't put it past him because he was a notorious miser. The only one he really spent money on was his daughter, who was gorgeous and kowtowed to the old man. Litzy wasn't sure, but if she didn't know any better, she would think that Rowland and his daughter had been lovers at one time. There were pictures of his daughter on his lap, and there had definitely been the signs of a hard-on in the shadows of his trousers. It was a disgusting thought, but one she did not necessarily refute. After all, she wasn't the only one who had such thoughts. Many of his enemies thought the same thing and would love to see him behind bars as an abusive father and a pedophile.

She took her pulse and realized her heart rate was lowering by the second, so she finished her drink, left money on the bar with a sizeable tip, and walked out headed for home. It was time to get some sleep. Rowland was going to do his magic, and she didn't have anything to worry about, except for the fact that he had something over her and would use it when he considered it the right thing to do to protect himself. He was scum. He ran an organization of scum. Now he was thinking of running for president. What a bad idea. He would destroy America if he could, maybe turn it into an authoritarian state, resembling the ones he admired. It was a scary thought, but one she could not get rid of so easily.

When she got to her condo, she slipped in quietly so she wouldn't wake up her next door neighbor, Nancy Evans. She went into her bedroom and proceeded to undress in the dark. When she was down to her bra and panties, she slipped under the covers of her bed, enjoying the luxury of sleeping alone.

9

The morning sun coming through the windows hit Mike squarely in the face, waking him up slowly but surely. He was disoriented at first, not realizing where he was. Then he remembered he was in the newsroom and sat up straight in his desk chair and stretched until practically every bone in his body snapped, crackled, and popped with satisfaction. His rear end was asleep, and he stood up, starting the blood flowing again to that part of his body..

Bob Fielding, a short, pudgy man in a bland gray suit, stuck his head around the cubicle entrance and looked Mike up and down and said, "You look like shit."

Mike said, "I feel even worse."

"What's up? You sleep here again?"

"You guessed it."

"You're making a habit of it."

"I know," Mike agreed. "A bad habit."

"Don't say I didn't warn you."

"I won't."

"What do you got planned for today?" Fielding asked.

"News conference."

"Where?"

"Rowland Enterprises."

"Eddie himself called it, didn't he?"

"You got that right."

"You know why?"

Mike put a finger to his lips and whispered, "It's a secret."

"Well," Fielding said, "I'll see you later. After you've filed your story, I guess."

"I guess so," Mike confirmed.

Fielding waved a hand and disappeared around the corner. Mike wouldn't be surprised if Fielding took up a post somewhere so he could spy on others and overhear some choice info. He was lazy and never felt like going out and drumming up a story. Instead, he listened to others and made up his own shit. He was a crummy journalist, and Mike wondered why they kept him around. Maybe for laughs, he thought.

He decided to go home and freshen up. Take a shower or something. Shave. Whatever. He left the building and took a cab to his apartment. When he entered, he could smell the fresh scent of his boyfriend, Jake Gottlieb. Jake came out of the bathroom, naked, his cock erect. Mike smiled.

"Were you expecting me?" he asked flirtatiously.

"Not really," Jake said. "At my age, a stiff wind can make me hard."

"Well, I wish I had time to do something about it, but I have to get ready for a news conference."

"Be my guest," Jake said, motioning to the bathroom.

Mike quickly stripped, made sure the water was just right, and stepped into the shower. He soaped himself up, but soon Jake was there, helping him. They helped each other relieve the sexual tension they both felt when around each other, then Mike toweled himself off while Jake brushed his teeth. Jake was tall and lean and strongly muscled; he was a trainer at one of the more popular gyms in the area. That's where they had met; Jake was his trainer at the beginning, but soon he was giving Mike blowjobs in the shower room when they were all alone. They instantly liked each other and became a couple soon after they met.

Now, they practically lived together, and they had no secrets.

"What's this news conference about?" Jake asked.

"Eddie Rowland's going to announce his bid for the presidency," Mike told him.

"You're kidding."

"I wish I were."

"Does he really think he can win?"

"He has enough money."

"That doesn't answer my question."

"Believe me, Jake honey," Mike cautioned, "I don't know what goes through Rowland's brainless physiognomy."

"Nicely put."

Mike put on his dark blue pinstripe suit with a red power tie and a handkerchief to match. He looked stunning.

"If I didn't know it was you," Jake said, "I wouldn't know it was you."

"Is that supposed to be a compliment?"

"Something like it."

It was 10:15 by the time Mike was ready to go. The press conference was at 11:00. He had plenty of time. One last look at himself in the mirror, a quick kiss for Jake, and he was at the door.

"You look stunning," Jake told him.

Mike had been thinking the same thing. He gave a farewell wave and stepped out the door.

10

Bobby Borstrand didn't sleep well that night. Julie hadn't come home. He tossed and turned, and his brain wouldn't shut off. All he could think about was the mess he had made of his marriage.

Not that he would have changed anything, but at least he could have been a little more discreet. He was a cockshound, he knew that. He couldn't control himself when it came to women. He had to conquer any fairly attractive female who crossed his path. He felt his power entitled him to use women for his own pleasure.

Ever since he had gone into politics at a young age, he had wrestled with his primal urges. He didn't want to give in to them because he didn't want to hurt Julie. But he really couldn't help himself. He had gone to see many a psychiatrist or therapist, asking them to find a cure for the problem. They put him through many rigorous sessions: he was hypnotized quite a few times, but eventually, none of it did any good. He still couldn't help himself when it came to women. And because of his power, he was able to conquer many young women who gave in to him simply because of who he was. It's good to be powerful, he thought, especially when it comes to women.

Borstrand's career in politics had been rapid and unconventional. He had been mayor of Little Rock, Arkansas, when he had decided to run for president, at the prompting of Julie, of course. He thought she was much more ambitious than he was; he would have remained mayor for as long as he could have before running for the White House. But Julie had other ideas: she wanted to be First Lady of the United States as a prelude to becoming the first female president. Then Borstrand would be known as the First Gentleman, and he didn't really like that. In fact, he didn't like taking a back seat to Julie at all. She was very aggressive when it came to his career, because she found it a way to confirm her own aspirations. So she was the first one to beat the drum for him, overlooking his many dalliances with women she did or didn't like. She just wanted to make the White House her home for a little while.

Borstrand got out of bed and wandered sleepily into the bathroom. He undressed, leaving his Jethro Tull T-shirt and his sweatpants on the floor for Melinda to pick up, and entered the shower. Without thinking, he turned on the water, and when the cold spray hit him, he let out a muffled cry. The water quickly warmed up, and he managed to take his shower quickly. He spent some extra time in the shower to shave. Then he left the shower, dried off, and then padded naked back into the bedroom where he dressed carefully because he had already heard that today was the day Eddie Rowland announced his candidacy for president, a day that would probably live in infamy as FDR would have announced. In Borstrand's opinion, Rowland was a prize moron; he was a megalomaniac who only cared about one thing: himself. Not that most politicians didn't care only about themselves, but at least they had the good sense not to show it. Rowland was so full of himself that when someone he was talking to started talking about something else, he walked away without saying anything.

Borstrand looked at his best when he was finished dressing.

He inspected himself in the mirror and was quite pleased. No matter what anyone said, he was a good-looking older gentleman. At his age, he managed to turn a few women's heads, young and old. If that was only because of his reputation, it didn't make a difference. At least, to him. He was still a cockshound and looked forward to the admiration given to him by women. He loved the feel of women, the smell of women, the sight of women. To him, there were no ugly women. They all coalesced into one breathtaking beauty of the species. As he had these thoughts, he had an erection, and he had to adjust his trousers so he wouldn't reveal it to anyone.

Borstrand left his bedroom and walked down a long hallway until he arrived at the dining room, which was laid out with food galore. Borstrand liked a hearty breakfast. He filled a plate and sat down at the head of the table. However, before he could begin eating, there was a sharp knock on the door, and it opened to reveal Sam Peterson, Borstrand's private secretary.

Borstrand would have preferred a female secretary, but Julie wouldn't allow it, unless she was someone in her 80s, and Borstrand did not want that, because he did have his standards and, when it came to women, age was important. Anyone past 60 was not allowed. Therefore, he chose Peterson, the perfect candidate; he had a solid resume and was fairly young – 35, to be exact – and was hardworking and energetic. That's why he came in that morning with his arms full of papers and his ever-present notebook sticking out of one of his side pockets. He was tall and thin and lacked a chin, but he was an attractive man in spite of that. He walked quickly to Borstrand's side.

"Good morning, President Borstrand," he said. "How are you this morning?"

"Just fine, Sam, just fine. How about you?"

"I'm doing well, sir," Peterson said, as deferentially as he could. "Just a few notes on your speech to the Ladies' Club this afternoon."

Borstrand eyed the papers in Peterson's arms skeptically. "Just a few notes?"

"Okay," Peterson admitted, "more than a few."

He laid them on the table next to Borstrand's breakfast plate.

"Can't I look at them after breakfast?"

"Whenever you wish, sir. I have some news, though."

"Spill it," Borstrand said as he bit into a sausage patty.

"There's a press conference today being held by Eddie Rowland."

Borstrand paused in his eating as if he was surprised at the news. He sat back in his chair. "Really? What about?"

"I'm not sure, sir, but there's a rumor that he's going to announce his candidacy for president on the republican ticket."

"No kidding," Borstrand said in his most laid-back drawl. "Eddie Rowland running as a republican?"

"That's what they say."

"Amazing. I would never have thought it."

"No one would, sir."

"Thanks for the news. Now let me finish my breakfast."

"Yes, sir," Peterson said with the shade of a bow, and he immediately left the room.

Borstrand smiled. Things were working out the way they had planned. The question was, should he go to the conference? No, he thought, it'd be better if he watched it on television. If he appeared at the conference in person, people would get suspicious. He needed to keep as low a profile as possible.

He bent over his plate and continued eating.

11

A few hours earlier, Rowland had disconnected the phone call with Litzy. Stupid cunt, he thought. What would women do without men like me? He called a particular number he had memorized. It rang a couple of times before it was picked up. A raspy voice answered. Rowland gave some instructions. After they were through, the phone call ended, and Rowland returned his phone to his nightstand. He lay back in bed, the one he didn't share with Carlotta, and tried to get some sleep. It was going to be a long day. He had to get some rest, at least.

***

After tossing and turning for another hour, he got up and got dressed and left his bedroom, and walked to his office, where he sat at his desk and started to make phone calls. It was only six o'clock, but Rowland knew those he called would be up and about. An hour later, his family was surrounding him, as was his best friend, Albert Hanson. They all looked at him expectantly. He sat back in his plush desk chair and smiled.

"I have some news," he said to them. He paused dramatically. "I'm going to run for president."

There was a bit of a gasp from some of the members of his family, especially from his oldest, his daughter, Priscilla. She was a beautiful young lady, blonde-haired, blue-eyed, with a body that would not quit. At least, that's what her father always thought.

And not only did she have looks, she had brains, too. She was quite a complete package, he thought. One of my finest creations. A work of art, in his mind. He was very proud of her, and he knew she'd be the first to get the ball rolling.

She leaned forward from where she was sitting across the room and said, "Are you serious, Dad? Or is this just another one of your advertising ploys?"

Rowland shrugged and said, "What would I be advertising?"

"Oh, I don't know. Maybe another one of your scams."

"You don't have much faith in me, do you?" Rowland asked.

"Oh, I have great faith in you. I believe everything you tell me. Until I don't have to believe it anymore."

She was a smart one all right, Rowland thought, brains and beauty.

Then his youngest son, Daniel, spoke. "What's all this about, Dad?" he asked. "You've never shown any interest in politics before."

"That's right," Rowland conceded, "but my interest in the world has finally expanded."

"So," said the middle son, Roger, "you're going to give Julie Borstrand a run for her money."

"No," Rowland said defiantly, and paused dramatically again while they were stunned into silence. Then he said, "I'm going to run as a republican."

Another gasp could be heard, but this time more audible and from everyone in the room.

"Dad," Priscilla said, "you can't be serious. After all, we've always been Democrats."

"That's true," Rowland said, "but I don't think I'd stand a chance trying to beat Julie for the nomination, so I've decided to go for it from the other side."

"You're willing to change your allegiance," Roger said, "simply to become president?"

"Why not?" Rowland said. "I wouldn't be the first one to do such a thing," mimicking the words of Julie.

"No," Daniel said, "but you'd change from being the biggest man in New York to being the biggest man in the world."

"That's right," Rowland said, with a smug smile.

"How can you get away with it?" Roger asked.

"Money talks," Rowland said, "and bullshit walks."

"I guess you're going to prove that," Roger said.

"You bet your ass," Rowland said.

"So what about us?" Priscilla asked.

"What about you?"

"What are we supposed to do?"

"What do you think?" Rowland asked aggressively. "You're going to run the business, and you're going to be my closest advisors."

"Hey, that's cool," Roger said. "Will we have offices in the White House?"

"I think I can arrange it," Rowland assured him.

"Cool," Roger repeated.

Rowland's sons were two of the biggest morons he knew, but he could use them for his purposes. Roger, the middle child, was short and scruffy, with a flat face and thick lips. Daniel, on the other hand, was tall and graceless, but handsome in a pretty way. His father thought he was gay, but Daniel wouldn't have the nerve to tell him. They were his tools, and he was going to use them appropriately.

At that moment, his pocket began to vibrate. He pulled the phone out of his pocket and glanced at the screen. It vibrated some more. He turned to those around him and said, "I have to take this." He stood and walked to the floor-to-ceiling windows, which overlooked his piece of New York City, the piece he owned anyway. He answered his phone.

The raspy voice told him, "It's done," and the call was disconnected.

Rowland put his phone back in his pocket and turned to the room. He looked at his best friend. "Al," he said, "you've been surprisingly quiet."

Hanson looked up at him from where he sat on the couch. "I'll save my comments for when we're alone," he said slyly. He was middle-aged and heavily built, with a perpetual unshaven and unclean look. He had known Rowland since they were kids and grew up together in Queens. He sat back on the couch and waited for the onslaught.

"What's the matter, Al?" Roger demanded, with a bit of a laugh. "Too shy to talk in front of the rest of us?"

"What I have to say, Roger, is none of your damn business."

Roger was taken aback. "If it has to do with the family, then it's all of our business."

"I'll leave that to your father. If he thinks he should share it with you, then that's his decision."

"Something's not right here," Priscilla said. Leave it to her to figure out what was going on. "What are you not telling us, Dad?"

"I'm telling you everything for the moment," Rowland said. "I'm telling you everything you need to know."

"That's an evasion if I ever heard one," Priscilla stated.

"Don't be so suspicious, my darling daughter. I'm turning republican, and I expect all of you to do the same."

"Adam's not going to like this," Priscilla said, referring to her husband. "After all, he's Jewish."

"Does that mean he has to be a Democrat?" Rowland asked. "I know a lot of republican Jews."

"And they're all oxymorons," Priscilla said.

"Don't be so sarcastic, my dear," Hanson said. "Jews have as much right to be republicans as anybody else."

"So you say," Priscilla said.

"I told you not to marry the guy," Roger said. "We didn't need a kike in the family."

Priscilla swiveled around to face him, fury written all over her face. "He's the father of our children," Priscilla spat at him, "and he's a good husband. Why don't you keep your fucking trap shut sometimes?"

"Okay, sis," Roger said, "it's your funeral."

Rowland intervened. "Children, children," he said, "enough bickering already." He agreed with Roger's opinion of his son-in-law, but he wasn't going to state it out loud.

"Dad's right," Daniel said. "We need to stick close together if Dad intends to take over this country."

Rowland looked at Daniel in surprise. He suddenly felt a new admiration for his youngest son, because Rowland hadn't thought about what he'd said before but was now becoming more akin to it. Things were looking up, he thought.

"Listen, you guys," Hanson said, sounding somewhat like Edward G. Robinson, "would you mind leaving us alone? I need to talk with your father in private."

"Okay, Uncle Al," Priscilla said flirtatiously, "just make it quick. We have a lot of planning to do." She turned to the door, swinging her expressive hips in a way she knew Hanson liked. "Come on, fellas."

Roger and Daniel stood up and followed her to the door. "That's right, children," Rowland said, "do what your elders say."

"Yes, father," Priscilla said, swiveling her hips some more and disappearing out the door, followed by her brothers, who looked glum and felt overshadowed.

When the door slowly closed behind them, Hanson took out a Cuban cigar and lit it. He let a cloud of smoke drift from his nostrils.

"Where do you get those nasty things?" Rowland asked, making a foul face.

"I have my suppliers."

"Don't you know they're illegal in this country?"

"I'm well aware of it," Hanson said. "That's why I only smoke them when I'm alone or with you."

"So I suppose you were happy when Grant opened relations with Castro?"

"To a point. These cigars are wonderful."

"I'm sure. You've told me enough times." Rowland pouted a little bit. "That black bastard pretty much ruined this country."

"Save that for when you run for president. It's surprising how you've bamboozled everyone into thinking you're a liberal."

"It was good for business."

"But now you're going to show the world your true colors."

"I plan to."

"You think you can get away with it?" Hanson asked.

"Just watch me," Rowland answered, and then sat back in his desk chair. "So what'd you want to talk to me about, Al?"

"Is your recorder off?"

"Of course."

"I don't want anybody else hearing this."

"No one else will. You have my word."

Not that that stands for much, Hanson thought. "So who're you getting for your campaign manager?" he asked.

"I was thinking of you," Rowland said.

"I don't think so. I have someone else in mind."

Rowland pouted some more. "Who?" he asked grudgingly.

"Frank Reynolds."

Rowland sat up straight. "Who the fuck is that?"

"Just the best man for the job," Hanson said. "He has all the right connections."

Rowland looked befuddled for a moment. "Connections?" he repeated. "What kind of connections?"

"The right kind."

"That means you're not gonna tell me."

"Not right at the moment."

"That means they're kinda fishy, right?"

"Does that disturb you?" Hanson asked. "Because if it does, I can always get somebody else."

"No," Rowland said hastily, "no, not at all. I was just wondering, that's all."

Hanson nodded. "Good," he said. "You're going to need him."

"Why is that?"

"Because you're going to go in with guns blazing. You're going to show those in the know that you mean business. You're going to open with an attack on illegal immigrants and eventually people of color. You're going to show them the true colors of the GOP."

"You're not serious."

"You wanna bet? If we go into this thing together, I want to see you win. I want to see you in the White House with my support. You're gonna listen to me, and you're gonna listen to Frank Reynolds; in fact, you're gonna listen to every one of your support staff, or you can find somebody else to be your stooge."

"But, Al..." He thought about the arrangement he had made with the Borstrands, and he knew they wouldn't like what was in the works right now. But he couldn't tell Hanson about it because it was a deep, dark secret. He liked Hanson's plan, but he had to object somewhere along the line.

"What?" Hanson demanded.

"Nothing," Rowland said timidly. "It's just..." And then he stopped again.

"It's just what? Come on, tell me what's on your mind. If we're not honest with one another, then we can't work successfully together."

"It's just that I've always been known as a Democrat and a liberal."

"Since when? Eddie, you've been known as a racist and a bigot for a long time now, and you're going to show it at the press conference today."

"Are you sure it's the right thing to do?"

"Of course, it is," Hanson insisted. "There are a lot of people out there who are dissatisfied with what's going on in this country. They want a change. In fact, they need a change. And you're going to give it to them. You're going to start a revolution in this country that will ignite a fire around the world. You're going to start something that will amaze everyone concerned. These feelings of racism and bigotry have always been there, but they haven't been exposed because they're not politically correct. To hell with that. You're going to fuck with the American people to such an extent that they won't know what hit them. You're going to take over this country until the rednecks and white trash rise up and take what they feel is theirs. You're going to be their white supremacist god. Don't you understand that?"

Rowland was taken aback by Hanson's rhetoric, but it seemed to gratify him in a way that he hadn't known existed. He was now ready to go on the attack, in spite of the Borstrands' cocksureness and belief that they were the next messiahs. He was going to show them that he was not just a puppet; he was going to be a man of the people. He was going to rule the world.

Then he came back to earth. He had made a deal with the Borstrands, and he had to stick by it. We'll see what happens in the future, he thought. We'll go forward with Hanson's plan of attack and take it from there. Hanson knew what he was talking about, and with him hanging on to his coattails, they could probably make it work. But he didn't want to get his hopes up too much; he didn't want to be disappointed. He was a puppet for the Borstrands, but he was a tool for Hanson.

"Well?" Hanson asked. "What do you think?"

After a moment, Rowland's face broke into a smile and he said, "I'm in."

They shook hands on it.

12

The man with the raspy voice put his phone away after talking with Rowland the first time and went to work. He assembled his crew and made it to the hotel within 30 minutes. The crew consisted of six men, including the man with the raspy voice, and five of them entered the hotel in intervals so they wouldn't attract any unwanted attention.. The sixth man remained in the car, waiting for them.

The five men proceeded to enter the hotel room where the dead man with the erection still lay. Before they entered further into the room, they slipped on their protective gear, so they wouldn't leave any trace of themselves behind.

They spread a tarp across the floor, and three of them proceeded to wipe down every inch of the room with antiseptic. The remaining two went into the bathroom where they did the same. They found the dead man's clothes and dressed him as carefully as they could, although his erection made a tent out of his trousers. Then they put him into a body bag, took the tarp from the floor, ran a vacuum across the carpet, and left the hotel room with the body draped over the shoulder of the biggest man of the crew.

They made sure no one was in the hallway before they left the room, and then they proceeded to go quietly to the service elevator. When it came, they entered quietly and took it down to the loading bay, which was fortunately unoccupied. Of course, the man with the raspy voice knew the layout of all the hotels in New York – from the most expensive to the most inexpensive – and while in the room upstairs, he had texted the man keeping the car running to meet them at the loading bay. They found him there, waiting, with the trunk open; the large man deposited the body inside the trunk and closed it as quietly as possible. They certainly didn't want to attract any unneeded attention at that point in their operation.

The driver took them to a certain spot in Central Park, where it was very dark and deserted because those with any sense knew not to frequent the park at that time of the morning. Before doing anything else, they took off their protective gear, and when the body had been removed from the trunk, they replaced it with the gear. Eventually, the large man took the body to an isolated spot, took it out of the body bag, and threw it unceremoniously on an isolated spot on the ground. Then he returned to the car, where he threw the body bag in the trunk and closed the lid, not as quietly as he had before. After all, there was no one around to hear it. He got back in the car and it drove away.

When the man with the raspy voice returned to his apartment, he called Rowland and spoke with him a second time and gave the all-clear, then he took a shower, and when he was nice and clean, he climbed into a bed with clean sheets and fell asleep within seconds.

13

The morning sun streamed through the grimy window into Julie Borstrand's face, and she awakened slowly, her eyelids fluttering open as they would in a fairy tale story. She sat up in bed and looked around her, noticing that she was alone. Then she remembered where she was, and she smiled, taking in her surroundings with a long, penetrating gaze. At least, she had slept well, and one of the reasons for that was that she wasn't anywhere near Bobby. There was one time when she had loved Bobby with all her heart, but that was a long time ago, and she had fallen out of love with him, but not in love with anyone else. Bobby could be sure she had never cheated on him. That was the only thing he could be sure of.

But when it came to Bobby himself, that was another story. He couldn't keep from getting his dick wet with other women, she thought, a vulgarity that came to her suddenly because it seemed very appropriate. From the first moment they were married, he'd started cheating on her. On the honeymoon, no less. He took one of the cocktail waitresses into a storage room and banged her brains out. At least that was the gossip on the grapevine. She didn't confront him with it until they got home.

Then she lowered the boom on him, and continued lowering it until she lost interest in him and his dalliances. Let him do whatever he wanted to do, she thought, as long as he was discreet. But that thing in the Oval Office; that should never have happened; the intern should have been dismissed right away, but if she had been, it would have given truth to the lie they were trying to maintain. As it was, she got a photo shoot with Playboy and a bunch of interviews on some of the more rabblerousing television stations. And Bobby was impeached by a republican senate, but fortunately acquitted by a Democratic Congress.

Such remembrances made Julie tremble with anger. Someone might say she still had feelings for Bobby, but whoever it was would be wrong. It's the humiliation Julie abhorred, the fact that Bobby had so little regard for her that he would cheat with anybody who had a slit between their legs. She threw her legs over the side of the bed and realized suddenly that she was still fully dressed. She hadn't planned on staying the night, but now she was glad she had. She got her first good night's sleep in a long time. Maybe she'll make a habit of sleeping miles from Bobby; it might do their relationship good. After all, she was running for president, and if not for that, she would have divorced him a long time ago. But she had to admit, he had his uses, and one of them was as a campaigner. He would be good for her. After all, a vote for Julie meant Bobby back in the White House, and she felt a lot of people wanted that. Not just felt but knew deep in her heart.

She went into the bathroom to make herself look presentable: combed her hair, put on some rouge and lipstick and eyeshadow, and then she was ready for the day. She entered the living room of the so-called suite, pulled out her phone, and pressed the button she was looking for on speed dial. In a moment, her assistant, Mary Riley, answered her phone.

"What's up for today?" Julie asked.

"A luncheon with the Women's Club of Long Island at one," Mary read off, "and then a visit with the Children of the Lost in lower Manhattan at three."

"Okay," Julie said. "Anything else?"

"Yes. Where are you?"

"I had some personal business to take care of."

"That doesn't answer my question."

"Tough," Julie said. "Now. Is there anything else for today?"

"There's a news conference Eddie Rowland has asked for."

"Really?" Julie acted more curious than surprised. "What time?"

"Eleven."

Julie looked at the time on her phone. "Two hours from now."

"That's right," Mary said. "Will you be going to it?"

"I don't think so. Eddie and I are not on the best of terms." A little lie that she would be happy to promote. "That's it?"

"Oh, one more thing. North Korea has dropped a nuclear bomb on New York."

Julie made a face, although Mary couldn't see it. "Ha ha," she said sarcastically, "very funny."

"That's just to show you what might happen when you disappear from the face of the earth."

"I'll be in the office in an hour," and she disconnected the call without saying goodbye.

It was surprising how many loyal subjects Julie had, even when she could be abrupt and out of sorts. No one seemed to take it personally; they just knew who they were working for. Julie had a temper that would explode at times, even though she never meant to hurt anyone's feelings. She was just a passionate woman, and instead of her passion displaying itself through sex, it lashed out at anyone who got in her way. She was now looking forward to watching Eddie's news conference; it would be a hoot. Everything was going as planned, she thought. She couldn't wait for the press to splash Rowland's face all over the front page and make predictions about whether or not he could ever make it as president. Political pundits were always the same; you could anticipate what they were going to say at any minute of the day. They were so fucking predictable. She couldn't wait to hear what they had to say. Of course, this particular sound byte would be restricted to New York at the moment, but shortly after that, Rowland would become a household name around the country.

On her way to her office, she stopped off at her place to freshen up a little bit more. She saw that Bobby was gone for the day and thanked her lucky stars. The last person she wanted to see at that time was Bobby, for he would bombard her with questions about where she'd been all night. She would have returned the volley of questions about where he'd disappeared to so suddenly after the meeting last night. She knew Bobby's predilection for frequenting a whorehouse in midtown; it didn't bother her anymore. In fact, she was glad when he could get his sex somewhere else and not with her. Her indifference toward sex was something she hardly ever thought about, but when it came to Bobby, she couldn't help it. That's why she tried not to think about Bobby; it was a losing proposition.

14

Early in the morning of that particular day, a lone jogger stumbled upon a dead body lying on the ground in Central Park, the groin area of his pants forming a tent-like figure. He took out his cell phone and called 9-1-1. Ten minutes later, a patrol car pulled up and questioned the jogger, who pointed out the spot where the dead body lay. The police proceeded to cordon off the area and called in the forensics unit and called for a detective. The lucky detective who received the assignment was Ted Brown, a big black man with a shaved head and a perpetual scowl on his rather ugly face that women found very sexy.

"What've we got?" Brown asked McGilligan, the youngest of the patrolmen.

"Dead body. Looks like a man in his fifties, with a bulge in his pants."

"What do you think the bulge is all about?"

"I'd say," McGilligan said, stroking his chin thoughtfully, "it's a boner."

Brown's eyes opened wide in astonishment, then he began to laugh. "You're kidding."

"I'll leave it up to the ME, but – without any prior medical education on my part – I'm gonna stick by my conclusion."

"You call CSU?"

"Fifteen minutes ago."

Brown looked at his watch. "I guess they're running behind."

"Or maybe they just don't think it's very urgent."

"Maybe," Brown murmured, and he walked closer to the crime tape. Then he stepped under it, approached the body, and knelt down. He gave the body a cursory exterior examination, then asked McGilligan, who had followed behind him, "No visible marks or contusions?"

"Not that I could see," McGilligan answered.

"Any ID?"

"None."

"So, a well-dressed man in his fifties, no evident violence upon him, is found lying in Central Park. Where does that leave us?"

"With fingerprints."

"Leave it for the ME."

Suddenly, Patrick MacGregor, a large, heavy-set man with a ruddy complexion, burst through the cordon. "What's he been telling you?" he demanded.

"Where have you been, MacGregor?" Brown asked.

"Had to take a leak," MacGregor explained. "Any crime in that?"

Brown stood and stared at him. "None at all. Good thing your partner here," referring to McGilligan, "was around to tell me what's going on."

MacGregor gave McGilligan a sour look. "He's just a pup. Doesn't know what he's talkin' about."

McGilligan remained silent.

Brown looked at both of them, then saw the CSU van pull up. "We'll talk later," he told them. "Right now, we've got to find out who we have here." He turned and ambled up the hill.

As he approached, Carl Van Schneider extricated himself from behind the steering wheel of the CSU van and climbed out onto the grassy slope. He was already winded, and his large, florid face was reddening even more as he moved to the rear of the van, where he was met by Brown.

"Hey, Van," Brown greeted him.

"Hey, Ted, what brings you here? As if I didn't know."

"The real question should be, what are you doing here?"

"Sterling is out sick, that's why I'm pulling this kind of duty. Not my first choice."

Brown smiled and shook his head. "By the way, do you always greet all of us the same way?"

"It's my signature," Van acknowledged. He opened the rear doors, with some help from Brown, and he huffed and puffed as he removed his carrying case, which held all the instruments he needed in the field, and lowered it to the ground with a loud clunk! He had a coughing fit then, and Brown patted him on the back until it passed.

"How's the no-smoking regimen going?" Brown asked.

"Not good," Van admitted. "My wife keeps waiting for me to die already."

"Trouble in paradise?"

"My little angel," Van said facetiously, "and I have always had our ups and downs."

"Did she take a big insurance policy out on you?"

"What makes you say that?" Van asked, with a feigned look of surprise. "We're madly in love with each other."

Brown laughed and slapped him on the back one more time. Without asking, he picked up Van's case and started taking it to the scene. Van didn't protest; instead, he waddled up to him, and Brown made sure his pace matched the fat man's.

When they got to the crime scene tape, Brown held it up for Van, who scuttled through to the side of the corpse. Brown followed him. They stood side-by-side.

Van looked down at the corpse and said, "What's that bulge in his pants?"

"We think it's an erection, but we were hoping you could confirm it."

"I can't confirm it until I get him on the table. Any sign of foul play?"

"Foul play?" Brown inquired. "Now that's an old expression."

"An oldie but a goodie."

"No," Brown said, shaking his head, "no sign of foul play."

"So we don't know what killed him."

"Not until you get him on the table."

"I guess so." With much difficulty, Van knelt by the body and opened up his case, and took out a thermometer. "Help me here, Ted."

Brown knelt beside him, and together they turned him over.

Van pulled down his pants and shoved the thermometer up the corpse's rectum.

"Isn't that another old way of doing things?" Brown asked.

"The oldest way," Van confirmed, "is usually the best."

When the thermometer beeped, Van took it out and examined it. He looked at his watch and turned to Brown and said, "I'd approximate his death at between one and two o'clock this morning."

"Did he die here?"

"It doesn't look like it, but I won't know that until---"

"---you get him on the table," Brown ended the sentence.

Van looked around. "Where's the damn ambulance?" he barked.

"It's on its way, I'm sure."

"You're more sure about things than I am," Van said, and he leaned on Brown's shoulder in order to get up. He felt his pockets. "I could sure use a cigarette," he said, and he started coughing.

Brown stood next to him and patted him on the back. "If you have another cigarette, you'll probably be the next crime scene I investigate."

"Oh, leave me alone," Van said, and he moved toward his van as the ambulance pulled up.

"When can you do the autopsy?" Brown yelled after him.

"As soon as I can," Van said over his shoulder.

The morgue attendants climbed out of the ambulance – two energetic, well-built young men – and Van gave them instructions on what to do about the body. The two young men hardly listened to him because they had done this many times before. They got a gurney out of the back and wheeled it over to the body.

Brown yelled to Van, "Don't forget to get me the results as soon as you can."

Van nodded, said, "Sure thing," over his shoulder, and got back into his van with some effort.

Brown watched him drive away and wondered how much longer he had to live. It was a sobering thought.

15

It was nearing 11:00 in the morning, and Rowland was starting to get nervous. Not that he ever got nervous; he was too much of an arrogant bully for that. But he wasn't sure how people would react to his throwing his hat in the ring. There were a lot of New Yorkers who didn't like him, and there were those who tolerated his intolerable antics, but he also had a large base of hangers-on. These were leeches who latched onto anyone with money and tried their best to suck their hosts dry. But the rich were not as gullible as that; they held onto their wealth with a tenacity that gave them the name of greed. And they proceeded to accumulate more wealth until they had so much money, they didn't know what to do with it, and so much wealth that they couldn't spend it within one lifetime, let alone two.

Rowland, on the other hand, had garnered much wealth within his considerable lifetime, and he had lost it many times as well. His father had started him off with a considerable amount of money, but Rowland had gone bankrupt, forcing his father to give him more money, and then, after another bankruptcy, more money, and more and more, ad infinitum, until he died. Rowland was a truly greedy little son-of-a-bitch, and his father knew it; after all, they were related, and the greedy gene ran through both of them until it was almost unrecognizable as the money flowed through their fingers with undisguisable pleasure and malevolence. How in the world Rowland became friends with the more liberal Borstrands is not known, but they were friends throughout both of the Borstrands' political careers, and now he was even going to help her get elected president. Imagine, he thought, the first female president of the United States. He was going to be a part of history, a part that would blast through the world like a historic bomb and would take over everyone's consciousness.

The thought almost made him cream his jeans. He became so excited. And he was going to be a part of it.

Rowland was finishing up the Windsor knot of his tie when he heard a voice behind him.

"Let me do that."

It was Priscilla. She had entered the room silently and stood there for a long moment watching her father fumble with his tie.

He turned toward her, and Priscilla walked up to him and proceeded to make his tie look presentable. He smiled at her with something like fatherly pride as she made sure the collar of his shirt was straight. She patted his tie and stood back. "There," she said. "All ready for your big moment."

"I've have had many big moments before," he said.

"But this will probably be the biggest you will ever have."

He nodded his agreement, then turned to the full-length mirror behind him and inspected himself. "Looks good," he said, "even though I do say so myself."

"You've never been one for false modesty."

"Why should I? The truth is the truth."

Priscilla patted his tie one more time and then moved across the room to stand in front of the floor-to-ceiling windows that looked toward the South side of Manhattan. It was a magnificent view that looked out onto South Ferry and the beginnings of Brooklyn and the Hudson River. Beautiful city, she thought. My hometown. Yet I hate it with a passion. If my father didn't represent so much of it, I could deal with it better. But he has to kick people around because it makes him feel big. And that includes his son-in-law, my husband and the father of our three children, all under the age of five. Thankfully, we have enough money for a couple of nannies because I couldn't handle it without them. Just an hour with my kids is enough to drive me crazy.

I guess I'm a terrible mother, she thought, but then I never wanted children to begin with. It was my father's idea as usual.

She could feel her father come up behind her and put his hands on her shoulders. She shrugged him off and said, "No more of that, dad. From now on, we're just father and daughter."

Rowland stood back, abashed. "What's gotten into you?"

"Nothing but the fact that I'm your daughter and nothing else."

"You didn't think that way when you were 16."

"I was a child," Priscilla spat at him, "and you took advantage of that."

Rowland shook all over. "Well, this is a kick in the head."

"You don't own me anymore, dad. I'm free and independent."

"Since when?" Rowland sputtered.

"Since I've had three children by another man."

"Who? That pissant. The only reason you married him was to get back at me."

"Why?" Priscilla asked. "Because he's Jewish?"

"Boy, you're on a roll today."

"Just leave me alone, dad, unless it's about business."

Rowland held up his hands. "Okay, okay, whatever you say."

"Good. Now I need to ask you an important question."

"Go ahead."

"Do you think this is a smart move?"

"What?"

"Running for president?"

What could he say to that except yes? After all, he had promised the

Borstrands to keep their conversation private. He didn't know of any way to get around it. Of course, he could tell her about the plan and swear her to secrecy, but that never really works out. She would tell her idiot husband about it, and before you know it, the entire world would know. No, he must be silent. He must keep everything close to the vest, or else the entire plan would blow straight to hell, and he wouldn't be able to stand that. He was at a point in his life where he needed something to rejuvenate his spirits, and this might be the thing he needed most. He would have loved to take Priscilla into his confidence, but he couldn't risk it.

"Why do you ask?" he said.

"Because I was thinking that at your age it might be a risky thing to do."

She can read my thoughts, Rowland told himself. She's a witch. He chuckled silently.

She could read his expression. "What's so funny?"

"Nothing. It's just that I have thought the same thing many times, but it's a risk I'm willing to take."

"Have you had a check-up?"

"No, why should I?"

"Because before you run, they want to make sure you'll be able to live through it."

Rowland moved away. "I don't need a check-up."

"They're going to expect you to get one."

"Who's they?" he demanded.

Priscilla smiled and said, "You're running as a republican, right?"

"Yes."

"Well, the Republican Party, of course."

"It's none of their business."

"Sure it is, dad. You're 74 years old. You need to prove to them that you have the stamina to maintain a campaign."

"Of course, I have the stamina. All you have to do is look at me."

"That's not enough."

"What do you mean?"

"Dad, you're overweight, you have bad legs, arthritis, rheumatism…"

"Okay, that's enough!"

"No need to get angry, Dad," Priscilla said in what she hoped was a reassuring voice. "I'm only telling you what they'll expect."

Rowland remained quiet, his expression one of a sulking little boy. "I don't need them," he responded at last.

"You need their backing, dad. You know that."

"We'll see…"

"No 'we'll see' about it. They can help get you elected."

"I don't need their help." He sounded like a spoiled little brat.

"Okay, dad," Priscilla said, "whatever you say," and she moved toward the door. When she got there, she stopped and turned back. "By the way, dad, why are you running as a republican?"

"Don't you think it's a good idea?"

"Why? Because trying to run against Julie Rowland for the Democratic spot would be disastrous?"

"Why do you always ask questions you already know the answer to?"

Priscilla shrugged. "It's a gift," she said, and she opened the door and walked out.

16

Mike Espinoza was early to the press conference. He was looking resplendent as ever, and as he looked around the lobby at the top of the golden escalators in Rowland Enterprises, he saw no one he recognized. What a shame. He was bored already. He took out his cell phone and scrolled through his text messages. Nothing of interest. He pointed the camera of his phone around the room at the assembled crowd and used his face recognition app to see if there was anyone around whom he didn't recognize. The face recognition app didn't pick out anyone of interest, but suddenly he recognized Marie Fordham from The Daily News. He wandered over in her direction, trying to look uninterested and seem casual about it, but he was bad at hiding his overt interest.

She saw him, turned to him, and said, "Mike, how nice to see you here."

"I thought everybody would be here today," Mike said.

"Why's that? Because it's Eddie Rowland?"

"Sure," Mike said. "He's always news."

"Or so he says himself," Marie responded.

Mike had a little smile on his face as he asked, "What are you saying? You don't like him?"

"How did you guess?"

"It's written all over your face."

"Look, Mike," Marie said straightforwardly, "the only reason I'm here is because it's an assignment. If it weren't for that fact, I wouldn't be ten feet near Rowland."

"Don't hold back," Mike said facetiously, "tell me how you really feel."

Marie looked at him closely. "You're in some kind of a mood," she told him.

Mike shook his head. "No mood," he said. "I'm just feeling good."

"By the way," she said, "you know what this thing is all about?"

Should I tell her or not? Nah, let her stew, he thought. After all, I've already got my column ready to go. All it may need is a little tweaking, but then I'll send it off into cyberspace where everyone can read it. I've got a jump on the other assholes here. Leave it to Pedro. I owe him my thanks. Poor guy, I wonder why he took a swan dive from the top of that brownstone. Or maybe he was thrown.

He finally turned to Marie and said, "No, I have no idea."

"Neither do I," Marie confirmed. "What's in that schmuck's mind now?"

"We'll soon find out," Mike said, as he snickered to himself. Inside, he was really a bad man, even though he could charm the leaves off a tree. But when it came to his career, he was all for himself. In a way, he was as big a malignant narcissist as Rowland. Well, it takes one to know one. I can almost figure out what Rowland's going to do before he even thinks of it himself.

Before he knew it, the room filled up with many people he already knew. Journalists, they were. At least, that's what they thought of themselves. Instead, they were hacks, working for the lowliest form of newspapers. They made their money off the misfortunes of others, or the misfortunes they had created themselves. How did we get to this point? he thought. The generation of today thought nothing of making fun of those beneath them. Or, at least, those they thought were beneath them. Reality TV shows that embarrassed those who were on them were watched hungrily by those who loved to hate. And it was only going to get worse: reality TV shows were blossoming like a cancer in the minds of greedy and unscrupulous producers, who didn't have to pay writers or actors, except those has-beens who appeared on them without showing any shame. They were all going to rot in hell. Of course, any person with sense – and they were becoming fewer as the years progressed – knew that there was no such thing as reality TV. A friend of Mike's, when in Atlantic City, stopped to watch a filming of The Real Housewives of New Jersey on the boardwalk. He was very surprised at how many times they reshot the scene they were working on, proving to Mike that his friend had no sense; they hadn't spoken in months, mainly because Mike wouldn't return his calls. Mike suffered no fools; he needed friends he could talk to without bringing up a new show that was supposed to be "realistic." Mike always thought of such things in quotation marks; it was the journalist within him. It was hard to believe, but Rowland – the fool – was on a reality TV show as well. He played a part not unlike himself: the ruthless boss who didn't shrink from firing those under him.

Sometimes those under him were played by those celebrity has-beens who had no shame. It was totally embarrassing. I don't know how they live with themselves, Mike thought. They were nothing if not greedy, and the more money that rolled in, the happier they were, until the moment the show was cancelled. Then they went into a tailspin that there was no recovery from except for Rowland, who continued his real estate shenanigans that reeked of corruption.

"Earth to Mike," Marie said, as she snapped her fingers in front of his face.

Mike returned from his thoughts, looked at Marie, and said, "I'm sorry. I don't know where my mind was."

"Not here, that's for sure." She leaned toward and said, "I've heard the conference is going to be delayed," in a whisper.

"So what else is new?" Mike said. "He'd be late for his own funeral."

"Good one. I'll have to remember that."

Suddenly, he felt a hand on his shoulder, and turned to find Harry Shelton there, steering him away from Marie, whom he considered a foe he didn't want to associate with. They found a vacant corner, where they took up residence to exchange information. When they had run out of information to exchange, they stood around with nothing much to say to each other.

Eventually, they became bored with each other and their surroundings, and wandered away, not saying goodbye to each other, nor really giving each other any sign of acknowledgment. They were on their own now.

17

Litzy Baker couldn't sleep. After all, a man had died while his cock was in her mouth. How humiliating. At least, for me, she thought. He doesn't care anymore; all his worries are a thing of the past. He's a thing of the past. Stop being so negative, she told herself. You're better than that. Sure, you're a whore, but you enjoy your work. You love to suck and fuck, and you love to have someone eat you out. Although, she hasn't found anyone recently, who was good at licking pussy. Her last great love, Adam Feldman, was a great pussy licker. She got wet just thinking about him. If she didn't stop thinking about such things, she'd have to masturbate, get it out of her system. But she could remember his long tongue snaking up inside her, touching all the right pressure points until she came hard, bucking and weaving, with her thighs clutching his head between them. The pleasure was so great sometimes that she thought she might go crazy.

Then Adam Feldman picked up and left, for that skinny cock-teaser, Priscilla Rowland, whose father was one of her clients and who was the terror of New York City. She was disgusted by him as a person, but he certainly paid well, especially when she let him come in her mouth. She was never turned on by most of her clients, especially Eddie Rowland, but occasionally, there were some who were able to get her off, and she wished that one or two of them had remained loyal customers and stuck around for a good long while.

But it was not to be. She enjoyed when she had the bed to herself, but she got lonely at times. She wanted a husband, and maybe some kids, but she knew that wasn't in her future. So she bided her time, bought some property because she had the funds for it, and let it accrue all the interest she needed to live on. Soon, she would be a very rich woman, and then she wouldn't have to allow some scum bucket to get between her legs. When she was finally able to, she would pick and choose those she wanted to fuck, and not those who wanted to fuck her.

There came a timid knock at the door. She got out of bed slowly, shuffled out of the bedroom, across the long expanse of the living room, and looked through the peephole. It was Nancy Evans, her next door neighbor. Nice lady, but sometimes tiresome when it came to having a conversation. Did she want to let her in, or not?

There was another timid knock. She couldn't sleep anyway, so why not? She opened the door.

Nancy stood at the threshold, all of her 5'2" height erect and unassuming. She was a pretty woman of 35 or so, but she didn't know it. She had extremely low self-esteem, and it bothered Litzy every now and then, but Nancy was a nice woman and was sometimes very good company.

"Hello, Nancy," Litzy said, her voice full of sleep that wouldn't come.

"Hi, Litzy. I'm glad you're in."

"Would you like some coffee or tea?"

"Tea would be nice," Nancy said.

Litzy moved from the door into the kitchen, while Nancy closed the door behind them and followed. Litzy set the kettle on the stove to boil and sat down at the kitchen table, and lit a cigarette.

"When are you going to give those nasty things up?" Nancy asked, aggrieved.

Litzy shrugged and said, "Does it matter?"

"Yes!" Nancy insisted. "You're young and healthy for now, but that might not last for very long if you continue your bad habits."

"I have many more bad habits than you know about."

"I don't want to know."

"I'm sure," Litzy said.

The kettle began to whistle. Litzy took out two mugs, turned to Nancy, and asked, "Earl Grey all right?"

"Sure. That's fine."

Litzy put two tea bags into the mugs, poured hot water into each, and returned to the kitchen table, where Nancy had taken a seat, and Litzy's cigarette smoldered while Nancy gave it disgusted looks every once in a while. Litzy placed Nancy's mug in front of her. Nancy took the honey jar from the middle of the table and gave her tea two spoonful of the sweet, delectable liquid. Then she let it sit there.

"Too hot," Nancy explained.

"Of course," Litzy said, and didn't do anything to her tea.

She drank it straight.

Nancy could be quite a handful sometimes, Litzy thought, but it was sometimes nice to have company.

They sat there in silence for a while before Nancy asked, "So, how have you been?"

"Very well, thank you," Litzy said, always remembering proper grammar when it came to such a question. She had been corrected by her teachers and professors so many times that she would never forget the right way to say it, "well" instead of "good." She was proud of herself for that. "How have you been?"

"Good," Nancy answered, and the fact that she had used the improper grammatical word made the hackles at the back of Litzy's neck rise up.

There was another silence.

Then Nancy asked, "Have you thought about what I asked you the other day?" suddenly.

No, she hadn't. In fact, whatever conversation they had had the day before had completely slipped her mind in one ear and out the other. She was obviously a very bad friend, although she didn't really consider Nancy a friend. Litzy tried her best to think back to the last time she and Nancy had talked. She couldn't. It was all a blur.

She looked Nancy in the eye and said, "No, I'm afraid I haven't."

"Why not?" Nancy asked peevishly.

"Because I forgot what you wanted me to think about."

Nancy looked hurt, then her face broke into a smile, and she laughed heartily. "Oh," she said, "you silly girl. How could you forget such a thing?"

"I guess it didn't seem too important at the time."

"What's more important than your health?"

"My health?"

"Sure. I told you I have two passes to a health spa upstate. I can take a friend."

"A health spa?"

"Sure. Why not?"

Litzy thought for a moment, then asked, "This wouldn't be some kind of rehab center?"

"No, silly. Of course not. Just a girls' week away. Massages, mud baths, steam rooms, all that good stuff. Wouldn't you like to go with me?"

Litzy shook her head slowly. "I don't have the time, Nancy."

"Oh, don't be silly, you silly girl. Of course you do. Or if not, you'll make the time. Both of us will."

"I don't know, Nancy," Litzy said, unsurely. "I have a lot to do."

"I'm sure you do. But I'm sure it can wait. Come on, it'll be fun."

Litzy thought about it some more, then said, "Sure. Why not?"

Nancy beamed. "That's my girl. We'll leave tonight."

"So soon?"

"Why not? The sooner the better."

Litzy finally smiled. "Okay. It's a deal."

18

Detective Ted Brown, with his ten years of service so far, hated autopsies. The first one he had witnessed had made him physically ill. He knew before entering the ME's space that morning that the autopsy of the middle-aged gent found dead in Central Park was over, but he still had to look at the remains, and it didn't thrill him one bit. There was the body on the stainless steel work table, naked, with his dick still at attention, a large V-incision on his chest and on down toward his genitals already sewn up, and it looked grotesque with the man's dead penis still pointing toward the ceiling.

The ME was at his desk writing up some notes while munching hungrily on a thick, bloody roast beef sandwich. Brown didn't know how he could stand to eat after cutting into someone's body and pulling out all the organs and weighing them and inspecting them and putting them back into the torso and then sewing it up so it could be buried. Just the thought of it made Brown want to upchuck, but he did his damndest to keep the contents of his stomach down. Not that he'd had much to eat that morning, since he knew he would be faced with another dead body, cut up to try to find the time of death and the manner of death and all that good stuff Brown needed to put an end to the case of the hard-on death.

Finally, Carl Van Schneider, the ME, looked up from his notes and found Brown standing in the doorway. "Hey, Ted," he said, "come on in. I got all you need to know about the dead body with the hard-on."

Brown stepped forward gingerly until he was practically next to the ME. "Glad to hear it," he said shakily.

Van Schneider looked at his notes. "Very simple: heart attack."

"No kidding," Brown said softly. "What about the erection?"

"Found some lipstick and traces of saliva on it. Sent it out to be analyzed. He was getting a blowjob when he died."

"No foul play?"

"None I could see. I ran the DNA through CODIS. No hits yet."

Brown looked at the corpse, then back at the ME. "Any hits on the corpse?"

"Oh, yeah, we got that. Name is Earl Lester, CEO of Lester Industrial."

"No kidding," Brown said. "Big shot."

"Former big shot. I got all the information you need right here," and he pulled out a sheet with all the corpse's information on it and handed it to Brown.

"Thanks, Doc," Brown said.

"No problem. Anything else you need to know?"

"I guess not. This looks like an easy one."

"You're not even going to look for the cocksucker?"

"No," Brown said, "why should I? The lady was doing her job and probably got the biggest surprise of her life. Why hound her?"

"Because this could be a case of manslaughter. She inadvertently produced the heart attack that killed him."

"Come on, doc, you know that's stretching it a little."

"You're not even going to talk to the DA about it?"

"Why should I? I'd only be wasting his time."

"That's for him to decide," the doctor said, putting an end to the conversation. He turned his back on Brown and returned to his notes.

Brown waited a moment, then turned away from the ME, crossed to the corpse on the table, noticed the peacefulness on the man's face: what a way to go. He turned on his heel and quickly left the place he wished he'd never been aware of. When he got back to his desk in the precinct, he took out the paper the ME had given him. It had all the information he needed to inform the family of the death of the industrialist. But he was not ready to visit the family and give them the circumstances of his death yet. After all, how do you tell a wife— if there is one—that her husband was getting a blowjob that led to his death? Maybe the wife didn't like to give blowjobs, so he had to go somewhere else to get his jollies. A lot of wives from the industrialist's generation did not like to suck their husbands' off.

Oh, well, he'd better start thinking of the corpse as a person, rather than who he had been. He glanced at the paper again to make sure he got the name right, even though he knew it by heart from having been a lifetime New Yorker: Earl Lester, one of those strange names where the person has two first names. But that's not important, Brown thought. What is important is what to do about him. An industrialist who owned half of Manhattan. He must have a wife somewhere. He looked at the paper again: Lisa, that's the wife's name. Doesn't say anything else about their marital status. Lives on 5th Avenue, of course. He put the paper aside; he'll get to it later. First, he had to call for an appointment with Marsha Lemon, assistant DA, one he was on good terms with.

He reached for the phone.

19

It was getting close to 11:00, and Eddie Rowland was getting nervous. It was rare that he got nervous about anything, but this time was different. This time, he was going to announce his run for the presidency, something very few Americans get the chance to do. He was excited and fidgety, but he had to stick to the plan he'd agreed to. Everything was going to come out all right, he was sure of it.

There was a knock at the door. "Come in," Rowland called out.

Al Hanson stepped through the door, and then locked it behind him. Rowland noticed and asked, "You going to kill me?"

"Why do you say that?"

"Because of the locked door."

"No, no," Hanson said, with a smile. "I just don't want to be disturbed while I get you ready for your big moment."

"Ready? How?"

"By informing you of what's at stake."

Rowland turned away from him. "I already know what's at stake. You don't need to tell me."

"Au contraire," Hanson said, with a smug smile on his face.

Rowland waited a moment, then said, "Well, go ahead. I'm waiting."

"There you go, Eddie, not at all the patient type. You've got to learn some self-restraint. You've got to be presidential."

"You don't think I'm presidential enough?"

"Not by a long shot," Hanson confirmed. "You're as presidential as a ham sandwich."

Rowland wanted to tell him that he didn't need to be presidential, that this was only one big scam, that he would run and then be beaten by Julie. But he had promised the Borstrands that he would keep the secret until his grave. He intended to keep that promise, so he didn't say anything to Hanson that would give himself away.

"Listen," Rowland said, looking him square in the eye, "if the people don't like me for who I am, then they can go fuck themselves. But I can practically guarantee that there will be a number of people in this country who will accept me for who I am and like it."

"You think so?" Hanson asked skeptically.

In the next few seconds, Rowland looked his old friend over. Hanson always looked as if he'd just rolled out of bed: his hair was unruly, he had a three days growth of beard, and his clothes were almost shabby-looking and did not fit him correctly. However, Rowland admired him for the great mop of hair he still had, which did not compliment Rowland's comb-over one bit, because next to Hanson, Rowland always looked as if he was hiding his baldness, which was exactly what he was doing. No one ever questioned him about the dreadful look of his hair as it swirled unconvincingly around his cranium. Whoever his stylist was, he should be drummed out of salon school and summarily shot.

"What else do you think?" he asked Hanson.

"I think you put too much faith in the assholes of this country. They're dangerous, and can be made more so by the means at our disposal."

"You have a proposition then?"

Hanson nodded abruptly. "I sure do. It's now up to you to get the population so riled up that they'll follow you anywhere. Remember, we have a lot of dissatisfied people in this country, angry people ready for a fight. You've got to show them you're on their side."

"How do I do that?"

"By being sure you show them your racist side."

"What racist side?" Rowland asked, innocently.

"Oh, don't give me that," Hanson scoffed. "Remember who you're talking to. One of your oldest friends, who has known you to make many an unfortunate remark about African Americans."

"Oh, come on," Rowland objected, "those remarks were in the heat of the moment."

"Well, keep that heat going, and you could become president."

"Are you telling me that we have a problem about race in this country?"

"Now you're getting the idea. Look at all the White Supremacists and neo-Nazis hidden in the shadows. It's up to you to embolden them to come out of the darkness. That's why you're running on the republican ticket."

Rowland was silent for a moment, then he said, "I'm not that kinda guy."

"Yes, you are," Hanson insisted, "and you're going to prove it today."

"How?" Rowland asked hopelessly.

Hanson put an arm around his shoulders. "Just listen to me," and he began to whisper in Rowland's ear.

20

Mike Espinoza stood in a corner, alone, away from the large group of reporters that was growing larger by the minute, waiting patiently for the news conference to begin, scrolling through his text messages and finding nothing of interest, when his phone rang in his hand. He didn't recognize the number, but he had nothing better to do, so he answered.

"Is this Michael Espinoza?" an unfamiliar voice asked.

Mike's friends never used his full name unless there was something to hide, so obviously, it was not a friend. But he became cautious and said, "Who's calling?"

"This is Detective Armstrong from the NYPD."

Mike stopped leaning against the wall. He shot up straight as if he were at attention and spoke with an obsequious tone of voice. "Yes, Detective. What can I do for you?"

"I believe you were an acquaintance of Pedro Armendariz..."

"Yes, sir, that's correct. He was a CI of mine."

Armstrong cleared his throat. "And just what is it you do, sir?" he asked.

"I'm a journalist. I work for The New York Herald Tribune."

After a slight pause, Armstrong said, "I see." He paused again, then said, "Did you know that Mr. Armendariz was deceased?"

"Yes, sir," Mike answered.

"How?"

"I was at the scene."

"You were?" Armstrong said, in surprise. "Then why didn't you stick around?"

"I didn't think it necessary at the time," Mike answered. "I hadn't any information to give you."

"Is that so?" Armstrong asked skeptically. "Well, your cooperation is necessary now. When can you get down here to give a statement?"

Mike groaned. "Do I need to?" he asked like a small child.

"Yes. And it would be best for you to do it as soon as possible."

"Okay, Detective. I'm in the middle of a press conference right now, but I'll be down there this afternoon at two."

"Good," Armstrong said, then gave him the information of the precinct to go to and abruptly disconnected.

Mike looked at his phone for a second, then raised a middle finger in salute and put the phone away. He glanced around the room and saw that the natives were growing restless. He leaned back against the wall again, when suddenly a door opened and Rowland appeared, looking as grotesque as possible, with his swirling hair as distinctive a comb-over as could be managed and a suit that was having trouble hiding his obesity. Mike took that in at a glance, and then he moved forward with the rest of the feral animals, pulled out his phone to record what was being said, and wound up at the back of the crowd, but not so far back as to lose anything that happened.

Rowland stepped up to the podium that had been prepared for him, and lowered the mike so that he could speak clearly into it. "Good morning, everyone," he began. "Thank you all for coming, even though I suspected nothing less." He was obviously reading from a prepared script, because he never spoke so well when he was speaking extemporaneously. "Today," he said, and he took a deep breath, "is a historic day in the life of Edward Rowland. And all of you know, that's me," he stated as an aside, and a small coterie of Rowland's following chuckled obediently. "Now. The reason you're here. Take this down carefully, everybody." He paused meaningfully. "I'm throwing my hat into the ring."

There was a shocked silence. They all looked at each other, wondering what that exactly meant. It usually meant a run for the presidency, but that wasn't Rowland's line. At least, that's what everybody thought. It could mean a number of other things, but what they were, nobody could think of. They waited for Rowland to continue.

After the initial shock wore off, Rowland continued. "That's right, friends and neighbors, I'm going to run for president."

The crowd actually gasped.

"In case you misunderstood my meaning," Rowland went on, smiling evilly. "I plan to become president, and when I'm in the White House, a lot is going to change. For instance, the border with Mexico is to be heavily patrolled, and I will build a wall to make sure that none of those people get into the country. Remember, they bring crime, they bring drugs, and they bring disease with them into the country. That is going to stop. I promise that I'll make it so those people won't be able to cross the border. My administration will be the strictest administration anyone has ever seen. I plan to rule this country with an iron fist. If you don't believe it, watch me." He paused meaningfully. "Now. Are there any questions?"

No one knew what to ask. Except for Mike. He raised his hand and was acknowledged.

"Does this mean," he asked, "you'll be running as a republican?"

"I'm sorry," Rowland said, "didn't I make that clear? Yes, I will be running as a republican."

Mike went on, "But why? You've always been a Democrat."

"That's right," Rowland said, "but I've changed my affiliation because I don't like what the Democrats have been doing to our country. It's slipping away from us, and it needs someone like me to pull it back together. You see, I'm a businessman, and the country needs to be run as a business. That's where I come in. My business acumen will be just the thing to rescue this country from obscurity. If not for me, this country will sink into the ocean. I want to make America the superpower it once was. We need to look out for the Chinese, because they're becoming more powerful than anyone ever suspected. We need to nuke them out of this world before they do it to us. Who's next?" and he looked expectantly around the room.

Mike had opened the floodgates. The questions came fast and furious, so much so that Rowland looked confused and didn't know who to respond to first. Mike, on the other hand, had stepped back from the crowd, pulled out his phone, and sent the article he'd already written to the paper. It would be out in no time, racing across the world on the internet. He had scooped everyone. He strolled away from the clamorous crowd, took the escalator down to the first floor, and strolled out onto 5th Avenue, feeling extremely proud of himself.

21

When the conference was over, Rowland himself rode the escalator down to the ground floor, followed by his best friend, Al Hanson. On 5th Avenue, his limousine awaited; he climbed inside, with Hanson close on his heels.

The limo took off, and Rowland finally turned to Hanson and asked, "Well, how'd I do?"

"You did fine, Eddie, just fine."

Then Rowland looked around him and asked, "Where are we going?" in confusion.

"We're going to visit your speechwriter."

"My what?"

"You know that speech you read today?"

"Yeah? What about it?"

"That was written for you. What did you think? It just popped out of thin air?"

"I thought you might have written it."

"Not me," Hanson said, defensively. "I'm not that good."

"So, what's this guy's name?"

"What makes you think it's a guy?"

"Because you wouldn't trust a gal to do it."

"You're right there," Hanson affirmed.

"So, who is he?" Rowland asked, genuinely curious.

"Just sit tight for a moment."

Soon, the limo pulled up in front of a glass and steel office building on 6th Avenue. They climbed out of the back seat and shuffled hurriedly into the building. They entered a private elevator, and Hanson pressed the button for the Penthouse.

Rowland was impressed, and as they rode up the scenic elevator, Rowland looked upon the city that was his. At least, he thought it was his. The people of New York thought differently; most of them hated his guts.

He smiled smugly and turned back to Hanson. "So, who is it?" he asked.

"You remember me talking about a young squirt by the name of Jack Mayfield?"

"No."

"Well, that's who it is, and we're on our way to his office now."

Rowland didn't ask any more questions. He was thoroughly confused, but didn't feel like admitting it to Hanson, who thought him as solid as a rock.

After a moment, the elevator came to a smooth stop, and the doors slid open. They were greeted by a man dressed in a butler uniform. He bowed to them and then escorted them into a large modern room of steel and chrome, where famous art was exhibited. Rowland was not an art lover, so he didn't know the names of the works or if they were originals or copies. Rowland was pretty sure they were originals.

Seated at a large desk by a window that looked down upon the beginnings of Central Park was a young, prematurely bald man, who immediately stood up and approached them with his right hand stuck out. He was tall and thin, with a waxy, limp face and an ashen pallor that would not improve since he never stayed out in the sun for longer than he needed to. "Ah, Mr. Rowland," he said, "so nice to meet you at last."

They shook hands, and Rowland was amazed at how warm the reception was from a man he had never met.

"Eddie," Hanson said abruptly, "this is Jack Mayfield."

Rowland didn't trust people who made him feel as if they were old friends. He managed to put on a small smile and nod in Mayfield's direction, but he didn't say anything.

"Please," Mayfield said, "come and have a seat."

He led them closer to the window and offered the sofa, which was against the wall nearest the desk. They sat down without another word, and Mayfield moved back to behind his desk and sat down in his ergonomically designed chair.

"I saw your news conference," Mayfield began. "It was great."

"Yes," Rowland said. "I understand you wrote it."

"That's right," Mayfield said. "And you delivered it beautifully."

"Thanks," Rowland said. "I understand that you want to join our campaign."

"I would be honored," Mayfield said hesitantly.

Rowland looked at Hanson, who smiled smugly back. Then he turned back to Mayfield and asked, "What do you get out of it?"

Both Mayfield and Hanson seemed to go into a state of shock. They were both frozen in place.

Then Mayfield said, "I beg your pardon?"

"Listen," Rowland said, "I've been around for a good long time, and I haven't met anyone yet who isn't out for something."

Hanson reached out and put his hand on Rowland's arm in a sort of restraining gesture. "What Eddie means," Hanson said, "is how do you fit in to the whole scheme of things."

"I can translate for myself," Rowland said. "I don't need any help."

"I was just trying to clarify things," Hanson said. "No need to get huffy about it."

Rowland ignored him and looked meaningfully at Mayfield. "Well?" he asked.

"Couldn't you see what I'm after from the content of your speech?" Mayfield asked.

"I heard what sounded like a bunch of bullshit about illegal immigrants," Rowland said.

"It isn't bullshit," Mayfield said. "I mean what I say. I'm sick and tired of these fucking immigrants getting into our country and taking jobs away from white people."

Rowland nodded. "I see now," he said. "You want to make America white again."

"Exactly," Mayfield said, slapping his hand down on his desk.

Now, Rowland began to wonder what he'd gotten himself into. When the Borstrands hatched their plan, he thought they probably figured it would be a simple game of cat-and-mouse. But now, it was getting more complicated than anyone of them thought it might be. He looked at Hanson.

"Well?" he asked him.

"Well, what?" Hanson said.

"Don't you have anything to say?"

"I sure do," Hanson said, "but I thought you wanted me to shut up."

"Not entirely," Rowland said. "Only at the moment."

"Now you want to hear my opinion?" Hanson asked.

"Yes," Rowland said, "give it to me."

"Okay," Hanson said. "I think Mayfield makes a lot of sense. I think we ought to hop on the bandwagon."

Rowland shook his head as he sat back on the couch. "So," he said, with a sigh, "you want me to be the first racist president."

"Not at all," Mayfield chimed in. "Besides, you won't be the first racist president. Far from it."

"There were others?" Rowland asked, dumbfounded.

"Plenty," Mayfield said. "It's up to you to reach out to those groups on the sidelines who feel as if they've been sidetracked and not given their due."

Rowland was curious, so he asked, "What groups are you talking about?"

"You know," Hanson said, "fringe elements. White supremacists. Neo-Nazis..."

Rowland interrupted. "But my son-in-law is Jewish."

"Only in name," Mayfield assured him. "Otherwise, he's as white bread as they make them."

"You really think so?" Rowland asked, puzzled.

"Your daughter wouldn't have married him if he hadn't been," Mayfield said. "Look," Mayfield continued reassuringly, "you're our only hope. You have to rescue this country from the quagmire it's sinking into. Without you, it's only going to get worse. Us white people are becoming a extinct. We've got to change that."

"And you think I'm the boy for the job," Rowland said.

"Yes," Mayfield snapped.

"Definitely," Hanson agreed.

He looked around the room as he thought of what to say. This is something he hadn't agreed to in the beginning. If the Borstrands had known what was going on behind their backs, they would be horrified. They will soon be apprised of the situation, he thought glumly. This was an opportunity he really didn't savor, but he had agreed to the plan before really knowing the purpose behind it. Now he was stuck.

"Well, welcome aboard," he said to Mayfield.

"Thank you, sir," Mayfield responded, "I am greatly honored."

They arranged a meeting time, when everyone who was anyone in the Rowland circle would get together and hammer out a plan for his campaign. But before that meeting could take place, Rowland would have to meet with the Borstrands and explain to them what was now happening. It was probably inevitable that things would have to change before they had a chance to seriously act upon their scheme. Hopefully, Rowland wondered if they might not scrap his run for president, and he could go back to his nefarious schemes to out-bilk almost everyone in the greater New York area.

When Hanson and he were back in the limo, Hanson looked askance at Rowland.

"What's the matter with you?" Rowland asked him.

"I'm just looking at the biggest damned fool in New York."

"What are you talking about?"

"You hurt Mayfield's feelings."

Rowland was astounded. "I what?"

"When you welcomed Mayfield to the campaign, you kind of pissed him off."

"How? What do you mean?"

"You shouldn't have welcomed him onto your bandwagon. You should have been glad to climb on board his."

"I thought this was my campaign."

"Not really," Hanson assured him. "You now belong to a conservative conglomerate that will run everything their way."

"And if I say no?"

"Then you won't be president."

"I find that hard to believe."

Hanson shook his head. "You're so naïve, Eddie. Where have you been living all these years, in a cave?"

Rowland slunk lower into his seat. "I guess I have. Maybe I should forget the whole thing."

"It's too late for that. You're stuck."

My exact words, Rowland. "And if I decide to do it my own way?"

"Then you'll disappear."

Rowland stared straight ahead into the gathering darkness.

Part Two:
The Middle

1

Litzy Baker watched the news conference from the comfort of her home. She watched that pompous ass Eddie Rowland as he spoke to a public that no longer needed him. However, the public so far were the people of New York. The rest of the country doesn't know him yet, Litzy thought. Wait until he makes himself known to the boobs outside of New York. They'll eat him up like candy. Rowland knew how to manipulate people, especially stupid people like those who lived in the Midwest. They would surely be taken in by the likes of Rowland; they would accept what he told them without thinking about it. Rowland was a Bozo, a clown the likes of which the rest of the country had not seen yet.

The thing that made Litzy uncomfortable was when Rowland displayed racism and bigotry that he had never shown before. She was surprised, as well as disgusted. She had never liked him, but now she despised him. She would try to never look at him again. He would no longer be a customer of hers. She hated having sex with him, and now she felt nauseous at having sucked him off time and time again. He was disgusting, and she needed to keep away from him. But what about his running for president? The man was a demon, and he needed to be stopped. She needed to stop him.

She took out her phone and looked for the lawyer she had used before. Her name was Emily Fuentes, and the thought of Emily representing her made her smile, for when Rowland found out her lawyer was Hispanic, he would turn red in the face and look about ready to burst. What a joke on a very despicable human being.

She called Emily's number, and it immediately went to voice mail. She left a message and said she hoped Emily would get back to her soon.

She put down the phone and started packing for the trip with Nancy; her nerves were rattled by the news conference, and she needed to get away. Away from Manhattan, away from her awful customers, away from Eddie Rowland, who turned out to be even more disgraceful than she thought. She hurried with her packing because she would leave with Nancy as soon as Nancy got home from work. She was ready to get away from everything, including her awful existence with men who thought of nothing but themselves. She was tired of servicing them. She was tired of her life. She needed a change, something she had never thought of before. She needed to leave New York City and find a place where she could live without restraints. She needed a life where she could express herself without fear.

When she was finished packing, she retreated to the bathroom, where she ran a hot tub for herself. She undressed and stood naked in front of the full-length mirror attached to the door of the bathroom. She admired herself because nothing was sagging; she was still as beautiful as she had been in her youth. She was still slim, no excess body fat. Her lovely face was unlined and still expressed a radiance that was hard to capture at her age. But she still gave off what could be termed a still life of beauty. Many artists had asked if they could paint her, but she refused everyone because she didn't want to be Dorian Gray in reverse; she didn't want to age in life, while a painting of her remained young and lovely. She wanted her mind to remain untouched, to remain as young as ever until the moment when she looked at herself in the mirror and realized she no longer held youth in her slim hands.

She slipped into the hot water carefully and immersed her body from neck to toes. The warm water was soothing to her frazzled nerves after having watched that fat pig Rowland express his true feelings. She soaked in the tub while her mind continued its unpleasant thoughts. She felt that Rowland was unpleasant to begin with, but now she saw his true colors. He was nothing but a racist animal, looking ahead to a time when he would rule the world. At least, that's what he wanted, to be a dictator, to have the people of this world bow down to him whenever he felt the need to oppress them.

Litzy never thought of herself as political. She really didn't like politics, but now things were different. She felt she had to work to destroy Rowland, to keep him from turning this world into a human dump. Rowland wanted to find another planet where he could live the rest of his life without having to worry about climate change or anything else like that. He wanted to move to his own planet in the universe, while the lesser people would remain on Earth, wasting away and probably killing each other, something he was definitely not against. It was still early yet, but she knew what she had to do.

Many people might think she was overreacting, but she saw something in Rowland's face on the screen that scared her. She saw the look in his eyes, the evil squint that he used whenever he didn't like someone. He obviously didn't like the human beings of this planet, so he would choose a select few whom he would take with him to start a new civilization. Maybe she was overreacting, she thought, maybe she was using her senses too much in order to fight against authoritarianism. She always felt Rowland was dangerous in some way; now, she saw it on his face, the need to overwhelm everyone with his desire to smash them. Actually, he could become another Hitler, but he looked more like Mussolini, the buffoon who ruled Italy, who counted Hitler and Hirohito among his friends, the Axis powers that tried to destroy the world simply by chewing people up and spitting them out.

She started the tub to drain, then climbed out and dried herself off. She took one last look at her naked body and smiled with recognition. She was a gorgeous woman, and she needed something else to sustain her, instead of a job as a sex worker. Sex-worker! What a joke. She was nothing but a whore, and she had already come to terms with that realization a long time ago. Her pussy for sale, that was it. Although these days, she used her mouth more than her pussy, because she was afraid of the men who pounded her flesh with their dicks, over and over and over again. It sickened her. She needed to find something else to do. She was still relatively young; she could move on. It surely wasn't too late. She would talk to Nancy, and they would come up with some kind of a plan. They had to. She couldn't go on like this.

She walked out of the bathroom and was suddenly grabbed from behind. The person who held her was too strong for her, and he moved with her swiftly toward the window. She saw it coming, and her eyes opened wide with fright. This was the last day of her life, she thought. She struggled to get out of the vise-like grip, but it was impossible. She tried to scream, but nothing came out. Her vocal folds were paralyzed, and she was unable to warn anyone of her perilous predicament.

The window was already open, and she kicked out with her feet to stop her forward motion. But nothing would help. Before she knew it, she was picked up and thrown over the windowsill. Suddenly, there was nothing beneath her to stop her fall. She plummeted toward the street, turning over and over until her head hit the asphalt with a dull thud, almost—but not quite—a distinct splat!

As the life drained out of her, her body relaxed into a fetal position. She was back in the womb.

2

After the news conference, Mike took the subway down to 14th Street and then walked the rest of the way to the precinct house. There, he asked for Detective Armstrong and was told how to get to his desk. When he reached the homicide squad, he asked for the detective and was shown to his desk across the room.

Armstrong was sitting at his desk with his coat slung over the back of his chair. He was a big, beefy guy, with a lantern jaw and a buzz cut on his nearly bald head. He looked up at Mike, then glanced at his watch and asked, "Michael Espinoza?"

Mike merely nodded.

"You're early," Armstrong stated. "Have a seat." Mike sat in the hard chair next to the desk, and finally, Armstrong turned to him and asked, "So, you were friends with Pedro Armendariz?"

"I didn't even know his last name was Armendariz," Mike said flatly.

"So, you weren't friends?"

"No, merely acquaintances. He was my CI."

"Confidential informants are usually for the police. What made Armendariz so important to you?"

"He fed me information," Mike said.

"What kind of information?"

"The special kind. The kind that helped me write for my paper."

Armstrong looked down at his notes. "And you work for the

Tribune?”

"That's right.”

"How long?”

"What?”

"How long have you been working for the Tribune?”

Mike had to think for a moment. "Seven years," he answered.

"That long," Armstrong mused. "But you're so young.”

"I started as a copy boy when I was 18.”

"Interesting work?”

"Very.”

"You like it?”

"I wouldn't be doing it if I didn't.”

Armstrong smiled and shook his head.

"Now, look here, Detective Armstrong," Mike said, "what am I doing here?”

"Answering questions, of course.”

"But what about?”

"Your relationship with Armendariz.”

"I didn't really have one.”

"Then what were you doing at the crime scene so early in the morning?”

"I had taken a walk. I found myself in the area. That's all.”

"Then you didn't see the accident?”

"No, I didn't.”

"But you knew the victim.”

"Not very well. I've told you that already."

Armstrong nodded.

"Do you think it was an accident?" Mike asked after a moment.

"Why not? Do you think it was something else?"

"I don't know."

"But you suspect something."

"I suspect nothing."

"Then why ask?"

"Because it seemed unusual."

"Did it now? How so?"

It was then that Mike told Armstrong everything about the meeting with Pedro, including the threat of extinction on Pedro's part from the Big Con.

Armstrong listened without interrupting, then said, "The Big Con, huh?"

"That's what he told me."

"Did you believe him?"

"He was too scared for me not to believe him."

"Okay," Armstrong said. "I need you to write up a statement, then sign it. You think you can do that?"

"No problem."

Armstrong gave him a yellow legal pad, and Mike proceeded to write out a statement in careful longhand so that the person who typed it up would have no trouble reading it. When he was finished, Armstrong took it to a stenographer. While Mike waited, he looked around him at his surroundings, the dilapidated office in which the detectives at that precinct worked their cases. The paint was scratched off in places, especially in the holding cells; the wallpaper was peeling, and the criminals who went in and out of the place were either screaming their heads off or calmly accepting their fate without saying a word. Detectives were typing up their reports at the end of the shift, while others were filing away reports from earlier cases. The captain of the precinct was in his office with the door closed, reaming someone out for a mistake he had made. It looked very uncomfortable in that office, and Mike turned away because he felt uncomfortable for the poor detective who hung his head in shame and said nothing.

Before he knew it, Armstrong returned with the typed statement and placed it in front of him for his signature. Mike signed it quickly, then asked if he could leave now. Armstrong gave him permission, and Mike stood up and walked out of the large room without looking around anymore. He went downstairs and out the front doors without missing a beat. Soon, he was on the street, breathing the air, his lungs bursting from the onslaught of impurities. But it felt good compared to the stuffiness of the homicide department. Frankly, it scared him. He had never been in a police station before, except as a newspaperman. It seemed unusual that Armstrong would have questioned him about something that truly did not concern him.

But he was only doing his job. Besides, Mike thought, why would Pedro jump off a building? Why would he kill himself? It didn't make any sense. It was probably Connor Binghamton who had him thrown off the building. Pedro didn't have all the money he owed the Big Con. Therefore, since the Big Con had grown impatient for the money owed him, Pedro had outlived any usefulness he might have held for the gangster. Mike wondered if Armstrong would pursue the information Mike had given him. It was easier just to pass it off as a suicide. Case closed. No further inquiries needed.

Mike stopped off at the Tribune office to check his copy and bumped into Terry Wainwright, the editor of the paper.

"Great work, Mike," he said.

"On what?"

"The story on Rowland. You seemed to scoop everybody."

"Thanks."

He started for his desk, but Wainwright stopped him by taking hold of his arm. "Just a minute, Mike. I need you to come into my office. We need to talk."

"About what?"

"You'll see," Wainwright said and led him into his office. When they were seated, Wainwright offered Mike a cigar.

The room already reeked of cigar smoke—the only place in the building that could be used for smoking—so Mike declined politely. Besides, he didn't smoke, and the smell of cigar smoke made him nauseous. But instead of saying anything, he allowed Wainwright to light up and blow an enormous plume of blue smoke. Mike gagged, but he was successful at concealing it.

Wainwright was looking up at the ceiling. He let out another plume of smoke and then said, "How long have you been working here, Mike?"

"A little over seven years."

"That's right," Wainwright said, nodding his head vigorously. "And you've done a damn good job."

"Thanks."

"I was so impressed by your story on Rowland that I want you to continue."

There was a pause.

"Doing what?" Mike finally asked.

"Following Rowland around."

There was another pause while Mike kicked this thought around in his head.

"You mean," he said, "you want me to follow Rowland's campaign?"

"That's right," Wainwright said, again nodding vigorously.

"But that's not what I usually do. I'm not into politics."

"Well, get into it," Wainwright insisted. "It's time you changed the direction you're going in."

Mike sputtered a few times, then said, "But why?"

Wainwright leaned forward. "Because this is going to be a big one. I don't care what anyone says. I like the way you treated Rowland in your article. I want to read more of that. The man is dangerous, and I want the entire world to realize that. We need to take a stand on this one, so it's important for you to know that the newspaper is 100% behind you."

"But why me?"

"It's very simple. In the article you just wrote, you showed your cojones. I want it to continue. Understand?"

"But where is this coming from? You already have a writer of politics on your staff. Joe Mendes. He's good. Why pick on me?"

"You want to know the truth?" Wainwright asked.

"That would be refreshing."

"Mendes has been on the scene too long. He's grown stale. I need someone who can give the political scene a new perspective. You just proved you could do that."

Mike stood up and walked around some. Wainwright watched him closely, but didn't say a thing.

Finally, Mike stopped in front of Wainwright's desk. "Does it come with more money?"

"Sure, and bonuses, too."

Mike thought some more, then said, "Okay. It's a deal."

Wainwright stood and held out his hand. Mike took it.

"Good," Wainwright said, "you'll never regret it."

Mike didn't know about that, but he didn't say anything in return.

3

Nancy Evans got home at around five-thirty to find a crowd of people gathered around the street and in the front of her building. The crowd was so dense, in fact, that she couldn't see what the attraction was. She tapped a woman on the shoulder. The woman turned, with an annoyed look on her face.

"What's happening?" Nancy asked.

"Girl jumped out her window," the woman said, then turned back without another word.

Nancy gasped, then looked up at a gaping window; she could see some policemen looking out, taking notes. She gasped again when she saw whose window it was. She tried forcing her way through the crowd, but many of the people standing around blocked her way and made it hard for her to get through. Finally, she pushed her way to the front of the crowd and stared at a white sheet covered in blood spread over what she assumed was a dead body.

She was hesitant at first, but then she gestured a uniformed police officer over to her. The young cop sidled over reluctantly, but stopped in front of her, with his back to her. Nancy didn't know what to say at first, but then she blurted out, "Who is it?"

The cop didn't turn around, but he said to her, "Lady from the third floor."

"Do you know her name?"

"I'm afraid not. Sorry, I can't help you."

"But maybe I can help you," she blurted out.

At last, he turned around and looked her in the eye. "What's that supposed to mean?"

She hesitated, then blurted out, "You see, I live in this building. I may know her."

The cop looked her over slowly and carefully. "What's your name?" he asked carefully.

"Nancy," she said meekly. "Nancy Evans."

The cop opened a notebook he held in his right hand, and with his left, he turned the pages until he stopped at one, then he looked down at her. "What's the apartment number?"

"Three-B."

The cop looked down at his notes again, then took her by the arm and gently pulled her away from the crowd. "Come with me," he said brusquely.

He escorted her up the front stoop and into the brownstone, not saying another word. He let her go first as they climbed the stairs. Nancy was afraid, and when they finally stopped in front of the open door of Litzy's apartment, she felt her knees buckle, and she fell backwards into the cop's arms.

An older cop stopped by and said, "I didn't know you had such an effect on the women, Marino."

"I didn't do anything, Sarge. When we got here, she just collapsed."

"Who is she?"

"Her name's Nancy Evans. Lives next door in 3-B."

Sergeant Millier thought a moment, then said, "Wait a minute. I'll be right back. Don't drop her."

Marino didn't know what to say to that, so he simply said nothing.

Miller, a short bulldog of a man, proceeded to go up to the detective in charge of the case and whispered in his ear. Detective Brown looked up and toward the door of the apartment. He went first, and Miller followed him closely. When he saw what presented itself on the threshold, he was not impressed. In fact, he let out a hollow laugh.

"Bring her in," he told Marino.

He turned and went back into the apartment to the bedroom, where the wind from outside the open window whipped the curtains around and made the room unseasonably cold.

"You done with the window?" he asked one of the crime scene techs. The tech nodded, and Brown said, "Then close the goddamn thing," bitingly.

The tech hurriedly closed the window, and the room became instantly warmer. Brown turned to Marino, who had lifted. Nancy fell into his arms and he was now carrying her. "Put her on the bed," Brown instructed him.

Marino laid Nancy on the bed as gently as he could, but at the last minute, her head hit the bedpost with a dull thunk! She still didn't wake up.

"Is she still alive?" Brown asked.

"Oh, yes, detective," Marino answered, "she's still with us."

"Then see what you can do about waking her up," Brown said, and returned to the living room.

Marino got a glass of water from the bathroom and lightly splashed Nancy's face. She woke up slowly, and when her eyes moved around the room, her face took on an expression of horror. She sat up and looked around some more.

"Where's Litzy?" she asked, obviously confused. "What's happened?"

Marino crossed to the bedroom door and called out, "Detective, she's awake."

After a moment, Brown returned to the bedroom and stood over Nancy, looking sternly at her. "I'm Detective Brown," he told her. "I'm in charge of this investigation."

She shook her head. "What investigation?"

"Into the death of the young lady who lived in this apartment."

"Who? Litzy?"

"Is that her name?" Brown asked.

"Yes. Litzy Baker."

"Thank you. We hadn't gotten around to identifying her." He became more solemn. "Did you know her well?"

"We were friends. Good friends."

"I'm sorry for your loss."

"What happened?"

"That's what we're looking into. It appears she fell out of her window. Her naked, broken body was found not too long ago."

There was a profound silence, as Nancy began to weep. The tears streamed from her eyes, but she didn't make a sound. Brown stood and waited, trying not to seem as uncomfortable as he was feeling.

Finally, he broke the silence with, "Miss, I need to ask you some questions."

The noise around them was restricted to the living room, so Brown motioned to Marino to close the door but to stay put.

The tears were still soaking her cheeks when she said, "We were supposed to go away tonight. For a weekend getaway."

"That's why her bag is packed?"

"Yes," Nancy said. "She was excited about it."

The tears kept coming. Brown knelt beside her. "Look, Miss ... uh ..." he started.

Nancy looked at him now that he was level with her. "Evans. Nancy Evans."

"Thank you, Ms. Evans. Now, do you think you're able to answer some questions?"

She nodded slowly.

"Good," Brown said reassuringly. "How long have you and Litzy been neighbors?"

"Oh ... about two years."

"And how long have you been friends?"

"A little less than that."

"So, you became friends pretty quickly, didn't you?"

"Almost immediately," Nancy said, as her body shook from the tears that were escaping from her eyes. "We hit it off right away. I didn't care what she did for a living. I just liked her right off."

Brown waited a second or two before asking, "What did she do for a living?"

Nancy hesitated, then spoke softly. "She was a prostitute."

Brown was surprised. "Really?"

"Yes," Nancy said hurriedly, "but she was looking to get out."

"I see." Brown stood. "Did she tell you about any of her customers?"

"Yes. Some of her encounters were very funny. We laughed about them over a bottle of wine. A girls' night, you know?"

There was another silence, then Brown asked, "Any customer in particular?"

Nancy whispered, "Yes."

"I need to know who that was," Brown insisted.

There was a momentary pause.

Then Nancy said, "Eddie Rowland."

Brown's eyes opened wide in astonishment. "Are you sure about that?"

"Yes. We talked about him a lot."

"Did she like him?"

"No," she said, the expression on her face turning ugly. "She despised him."

"Why?"

"He was crude and uncultured. She didn't like that."

Crude and uncultured? What kind of prostitute was she?

He moved to the window and looked out. They were taking the body away. He watched as they trundled her into the coroner's van. After it drove away, he turned back to Nancy, whose head hung low and despondent.

"Are you all right?" Brown asked her.

Nancy nodded silently.

"Is it okay to continue?"

She nodded again, this time with a sniffle or two. Brown handed her a box of tissues from the dresser. She thanked him and took one and blew her nose. She took another tissue to wipe up the remains.

"Where did she usually go with her ... customers?" Brown asked.

"To a hotel. They were pretty well off, so it was usually a nice place."

"Where, for instance?"

She thought for a second, then said, "The Pierre. The Hilton."

"Any more places you can remember?"

"No, I'm sorry. I'm afraid not."

"That's okay," Brown said reassuringly. "Don't worry about it. You're doing great."

"Thank you," she said, taking another swipe at her dripping nose.

Brown continued to ask questions, some seemingly irrelevant, but he received no more new information. He released her and let Marino escort her to her apartment. He stood for a while, thinking about what she'd told him, and trying to piece things together, but it wasn't fitting correctly in his mind. He walked into the living room, just as Marino was returning from next door.

The crime scene techs were packing up. They moved out quickly and efficiently, and didn't say a word to Brown.

Marino came up to him. "That was a real fine job you did there, Detective."

Brown was distracted. He said, "Huh?" stupidly.

"The Q & A with the girl," Marino said.

"Oh, yeah. Thanks."

Brown stood there some more, staring into space. Marino stood there with him, not knowing what to do or say.

Finally, Brown turned to him and said, "You can go, Marino."

"Thanks a lot, Detective. I'll catch you at the house."

"You got it."

Marino left in a hurry, trying very hard to forget the discomfort of the situation.

Brown stood there for another couple of moments. Thinking. Thinking that something was off about this one, but he couldn't put his finger on it. Maybe if he slept on it, he would have a fresh mind in the morning. He needed some sleep, after all. He hadn't been sleeping well for some time now. Frankly, he needed to get laid. Masturbation just wasn't doing it for him. He needed a woman to lay in his arms.

He knew just the place to go to.

4

Earlier that day, Detective Armstrong was sitting at his desk, his lantern jaw resting on the palm of his hand, thinking about poor Pedro, the CI of that reporter. It seemed very unusual to him that the reporter would be there just around the time Pedro fell to his death. But the reporter mentioned something about the Big Con and Pedro owing him money and how he was sort of in arrears to the gangster, so maybe he would pay a call on Binghamton to see where he stood on such a thing. Of course, Pedro's death looked as if it could be a suicide, but then again, Armstrong didn't believe it for a second. After all, when Binghamton was involved, something was bound to happen.

So, Armstrong grabbed his partner, Felix Hernandez, almost kidnapped him from the break room where Felix was about ready to feast on a Subway sandwich, dragged him to their car, practically threw him inside, and roared away from the precinct house. Felix wanted to know what Armstrong was going on that he had to be strong-armed from a sandwich he was looking forward to, and driven God knows where. When Armstrong told him where they were going, Hernandez almost threw open his door and jumped out; he wanted to go back to the house.

"What's the matter, Felix?" Armstrong asked. "You afraid of the Big Con?"

"You bet your ass I am," Felix said. "I'd rather stay away from trouble instead of inviting it into my immediate area."

Felix had gotten his master's degree in criminal justice from NYU, and he enjoyed showing off his "superior intelligence." But he could be brutally honest about things, and this time he was being brutally honest. The Big Con was no one to mess around with; he was a psychopathic killer who had risen within the ranks of the Irish mob. If he needed to eliminate his own mother from the scene, he wouldn't hesitate to do it, and he wouldn't shed a tear. He was definitely someone to be scared.

Even with Armstrong's muscles and his gun, he was a little reticent about approaching the Big Con, but he had a lead to follow; he just hoped he would survive the evening. He did his best to calm Hernandez's nerves before they got to the restaurant on 9th Avenue, the heart of Hell's Kitchen. Armstrong was glad this was taking place in the middle of the day instead of the night, which could have been precarious for both of them. Hernandez wanted to stay in the car; Armstrong had to do a lot of persuading to get Hernandez to come along. And still, Hernandez walked six steps behind his partner.

They walked through the door into a darkened exterior. It took a while for their eyes to get accustomed to the absence of light. Once they were, they walked to the bar, which ran along the right side of the long, narrow room. There were very few customers at this time of the day, and when they flashed their badges, the bartender shrugged. He had a lot of hair, which hung down to his shoulders, and a handlebar moustache. Surprisingly.

"You didn't need to show those," he said, with a lilting Irish accent. "I could tell you were cops when you came through the door."

"You fresh off the boat?" Armstrong asked.

"No. I've been here for five years. Got my American citizenship and everything."

"Good for you," Armstrong said. "Now, where's the Con?"

"He's not here," the bartender said.

"Felix, get his name."

"What's that for?"

"I want to nail you when you lie to me again." The bartender said nothing in response. "Now, where is he?" Armstrong asked again.

"In the back," the bartender answered sullenly.

"Do I need you to announce us? Or can we just go back?" Armstrong smiled as the bartender gave another shrug. "I'll take that as a yes," Armstrong said, and moved toward the back office, with Hernandez shuffling behind him.

Hernandez was amazed at Armstrong, the way he kept his cool in any situation. Hernandez was about ready to faint, and he knew it.

When they reached the office door, Armstrong opened it without knocking. Hernandez swallowed hard as he followed him inside.

Sitting behind the desk was Connor Binghamton, aka the Big Con, a broad-shouldered, barrel-chested, barrel-bellied specimen of the species known as Irish gangsters. He was in his mid-fifties, with a creased but still handsome face, blond hair thinning on top, and a perpetual sneer. He looked up when the two detectives walked in, and the sneer increased. He was obviously not very happy to see them. He remained seated as they crossed the room to stand in front of him.

"Hello, Con," Armstrong said jovially.

"What do you guys want?" Con said, with a sneer in his voice.

"Some information," Armstrong said.

"I don't got any for you," Binghamton said. "Now, get out."

"There's a rumor floating around that you threw someone off the roof the other night."

"Not me."

"Well, of course it wasn't you. One of your goons, maybe?"

"The guys who work for me are good boys. No trouble."

Armstrong shook his head. "That's hard to believe," he said. "Your boys all carry guns."

"So? New York's a dangerous city. You need to carry a gun to protect yourself."

"But you also need to carry a permit to carry a concealed weapon, and none of your boys have permits."

"How you know that? You frisk 'em all?"

"Enough of your boys have come through the precinct for me to know better. I don't mean to be rude, Con, but your boys are a bunch of troublemakers."

Binghamton looked over at Hernandez and sneered some more. "Don't your boyfriend say anything?"

"He just observes," Armstrong said.

"Well, observe this. I don't know nothin' about no guy being dead. You have to look some other place," and he dismissed them with a wave of his hand.

Hernandez finally stepped forward, having gained back some nerve. "It isn't as easy as that, Mr. Binghamton. A man is dead, a possible suicide, but we need to know for sure."

"Ah, he talks," Conway said. "If the guy offed himself, why come to me?"

"Because someone told us you had a hand in it," Hernandez said.

"And who might that be?"

"You know we can't tell you that."

"Then I ain't talking about anything, and both of you can get the fuck out."

"My, my," Armstrong said. "Such language."

"It ain't nothin' you ain't heard before."

"That may be so," Armstrong continued, "but still, let's keep this conversation civil."

Binghamton stood up, all 6'6" of him. Both detectives had to look up at him. "So, you want to be civil, do you? I told you before, I don't know nothin' about any dead guy. Now get out of here. Is that civil enough for you?"

"That'll do," Armstrong said. "Sorry to have bothered you."

Binghamton nodded at them, and the detectives turned and quickly moved out of the office and through the bar and outside onto the sidewalk. They both let out a breath neither of them knew they had been holding.

Armstrong looked at Hernandez. "Okay?" he said.

Hernandez smiled. "Okay." He was just very glad to be out of there.

They went to their car, and Hernandez took over the driving. Armstrong sat hunched over in the passenger seat.

"So, what do you think?" he finally said.

"About what?"

"Binghamton."

"I think he lies through his teeth."

"Lying comes naturally to him."

"So, what do we do now?"

"I don't know."

They were silent for the rest of the way to the precinct.

5

Later on that afternoon, Rowland was sitting in his living room, watching Fox News, which was showing his speech over and over again, making him smile with glee every time, when his wife, Carlotta, entered the room and glared at him.

"So, you finally did it," she spat out. "You finally stepped into some serious shit."

Rowland, who didn't hear a word she said, spoke excitedly. "You see this, honey? You see my speech? Isn't it great?"

"Of course, I saw your speech. You can't help it. It's all there is on the news."

"Yep. Just the way I like it."

"Well, I don't like it. I want you to put this silliness behind you and move on."

Rowland muted the television. "I beg your pardon?"

"You heard me. You've made enough of a fool of yourself over all this. It's time to bow out and go on with your sleazy real estate deals."

Rowland stood up from the plush sofa and turned to face her. "You obviously didn't listen to what I said."

"I heard every word. Your bigoted and racist remarks were disgusting."

"I don't think so," Rowland said, looking her straight in the eyes. "A lot of people feel the way I do, and a lot of them will support me."

"A lot of lowlife white trash. I thought you were better than that."

"Well, I'm not, okay? I want to clean up this country and make it white again."

"Are you insane?" Carlotta cried. "What kind of nonsense is that?"

"The kind that will get me elected."

Carlotta paused before saying, "You're really serious about this."

"You bet your ass I am."

"Leave my ass out of this. You haven't touched it in a long time, and you never will again."

Rowland thought about that. "I thought we had an understanding."

"The understanding was all on your side."

"So, why don't you divorce me then?"

"And get nothing for all these years of hardship?"

"Oh, yeah," Rowland said sarcastically. "You've suffered all right. Living in the lap of luxury."

"If I divorce you, you're going to have to pay alimony and child support."

"Child support?"

"Yes," Carlotta snapped. "Have you forgotten about our son?"

"No, I haven't forgotten about him. So, if you divorce me, you'll never see him again."

"You can't do that..."

"Oh, yes, I can, and I will. I've got the money to do anything I want."

She snarled, "Oh, you fucking prick," and the spittle from her words managed to travel across the room right onto Rowland's face.

He wiped it off with the back of his hand. "That wasn't nice, Carlotta."

"What do you know about being nice?"

"You know, some people were wondering why you weren't there for my speech."

"It's simple. I didn't want to be there."

"You must have watched it."

"Yes, and I hated every word of it."

"You must hate me, then."

"You know that already."

There was a silence.

Rowland wandered away to the big window overlooking the city. "My domain," he said. "My city."

"You think."

He turned back to her. "What is wrong with you? Don't you want to be First Lady?"

"No."

"Why not?"

"Because I don't come from this country. It would be a lie."

Rowland came toward her. "You're my wife," he stated grimly. "You'd be my First Lady."

She smiled. "Do you really want to be president?"

"I think I can win."

"You didn't answer my question."

There was a pause. Then he said, "Yes, I would like to be president."

"Do you know what a hard job it is?"

"I think I'm aware of it."

"No, I don't think you are," Carlotta said. "You'll have to work. You won't be able to rely on your children anymore."

"My children will be coming with me."

That was a shock. It showed on Carlotta's face.

"But none of you are politicians," she said. "You've never been in politics."

"So what? I'm an American citizen. I'm entitled to run."

"Nobody likes you, Eddie. You're a despicable human being. In fact, I wouldn't call you a human being at all. You're a slimy worm. You're like a Mafia boss. You run an illicit organization. I know of a few people who disappeared from this world because they didn't agree with you. Is that what you do with your enemies? Rub them out? Is that the phrase? I despise you, Eddie. You're everything I hate in this world. I'm disgusted by you. If I didn't need you, I'd divorce you in a minute."

"Well, I need you, too, baby, if I plan to be president."

"What's that mean?" Carlotta asked suspiciously.

"Unmarried men are not good prospects for the job of president. That's why I need you. In order to make me look respectable."

"I've tried that for the 12 years we've been married. It hasn't done one bit of good. You're still disgusting."

"Are you through?"

She didn't say anything in response. She just crossed her arms and looked him in the eyes to show no fear. Because she wasn't afraid of him. That had gone a long time ago, along with his manhood. He couldn't get it up anymore. Not that she wanted to have sex with him anytime in the future. She just wanted to be left alone to raise her child without the interference of such a ruthless pig as Eddie Rowland. It made her sick just to look at him.

Rowland took a step toward her. "Now, listen to me," he said slowly. "You will be my wife while I'm in the White House. You will continue to show deference to me. You will hold my hand when we are in public..."

She shuddered at the thought."...and we will continue to be a happy family," he continued, "or else you will disappear just like those others you mentioned."

She glared at him. "Is that a threat?"

"Take it as you please. Now get out of my sight," and he turned his attention back to the TV.

After a moment of fuming indignity, she turned on her heel and stomped out of the room.

Rowland turned after she left and smiled to himself. He didn't think he would act this way, but his ego was getting the better of him. He would still play the game as laid down by the Borstrands, but then he would turn around and use his nastiness in all its glory to ride him right into the White House. He was getting to like this publicity and this action all around him. He knew he was getting a strong bunch of guys behind him, so he knew they could help him move forward with his conservative and racist ticket. He had always been a Democrat, but he hated what was happening to this country by the wimps. This country needed a strong leader, someone who knew how to run a country just like he would run a business.

Rowland felt triumphant so far; he was glorying already in his run for president. Now, he would be able to get rid of all those lousy foreigners, especially the Mexicans, and close down the border to the south. In fact, he would promise to build a wall there; he knew a number of republicans who agreed with him. He wanted to make America white again; he wanted it the way it was when the Pilgrims landed and tried to get rid of the American Indians. Even Andrew

Jackson agreed with that, and the author of The Wizard of Oz, L. Frank Baum. Both patriots, and he would show his own patriotism to the American people, so that they would follow him gladly into the jaws of victory. He was very proud of himself. He would show those who didn't like them where they could get off. Fuck 'em all, he thought, they deserve whatever they get. He'll show them. He will bury them, just like Krushchev said, and he will use the current president of Russia to do it.

6

Later on that day, Detective Brown was sitting at his desk, when his telephone rang. He answered right away. It was Carl Van Schneider, the ME.

"Got a break in the erection case," he said.

"The what?"

"You know, the guy who was found in Central Park with a big boner."

"Oh, yeah," Brown said, suddenly remembering. "What've you got?" He was listening very intently because he was distracted by some paperwork on another case.

"You know, that stiff who just came in? The naked lady who took a flight out her window."

"Okay," Brown said slowly. "What's that got to do with Mr. Stiff Cock?"

"Her spit was on his dick. She obviously didn't clean up all the way."

Brown sat up straight. "You're kidding," he said, a smile starting to crease his handsome/ugly face.

"Now, would I kid you about a thing like that?"

"What's her name again?"

"Litzy Baker. Classy name."

"Semi-classy, if you ask me."

The ME chuckled. "So, did I brighten your day?"

"You certainly put me in a better mood."

"What are you gonna do now?"

"Special detective techniques."

"Fuck you," the ME said dispiritedly, and the connection was instantly broken.

Brown laughed to himself, and then looked around to see if the captain was in his office. When he saw that the captain was indeed behind his desk, he got up from his own desk and shuffled over there. He knocked on the closed door and was told to come in. He pushed his way inside and stood before the captain's desk.

Captain Delaney was a bulldog-faced man of 55, thin on top but hairy around the chin and upper lip. He worked out regularly, so his physique was still almost as good as it had been when he was 25. Now, he was slower and more sedate, and enjoyed being behind a desk and not out on the street. Especially glad about it was his wife, Emily, of 20 years. She didn't want some rookie cop coming to the front door to tell her her husband was dead. She loved being the wife of a captain in the NYPD. She didn't want to lose the eclat that went with it, so she was very happy her husband was doing desk duty, running his own precinct. It felt good, and she was now satisfied with her life.

The captain looked up from his computer at Brown and said, "I'm glad you came in, Brown. I want to introduce you to your new partner."

Brown shook his head and said, "Captain, we've been through this many times before. I don't need a partner."

"You need one if you intend to stay alive."

"I'm better on my own."

"You'll be even better with a partner." He looked around Brown at the squad room and called out, "McKenzie. Get in here."

A distant voice said, "Yes, sir."

And in a moment, a young, handsome, clean-shaven man entered, erect in his stance, blue eyes shining with anticipation. He looked fresh out of the academy, but he couldn't be, Brown thought, if he had already made it to detective.

McKenzie smiled at Brown and said, "Hi. How ya doin'?" He had a definite Brooklyn accent, which grated significantly on Brown's nerves.

Brown was born and raised in Manhattan, and, therefore, had no accent that anyone could trace.

"McKenzie," the captain started, "this is Brown..."

Before he could finish, McKenzie eagerly held out his hand. "Nice to meetcha," he said.

"Can I finish?" the captain asked.

McKenzie took his hand out of Brown's grip and seemed to stand more at attention than before. "Sure, captain," he said. "Sorry."

"No apologies necessary," the captain growled insincerely. "You two are now partners. I give you my blessing."

McKenzie smiled some more, which was another thing that grated on Brown's nerves; he didn't like constant smilers.

"Glad to have you aboard," Brown said to McKenzie, grudgingly.

"That's nice," the captain said, with a big grin. "I'm glad to see you two getting along so well. Now, get lost." He returned to his computer.

Brown took a step forward. "I have some information, sir, about the woman whose body was found on the street outside her apartment."

"Oh, yeah," the captain sneered. "And just what might that be?" he asked as he continued to play around with his computer.

"Remember the guy we found who had a perpetual hard-on?"

"Yeah? What about him? Did his dick finally go down?" he asked, with a salacious smirk.

"No, sir," Brown answered, "but the woman's saliva was found on it."

The captain stopped typing suddenly and looked up. "No kidding? What's the connection?"

"Well, since Litzy Baker was a prostitute, I think we can safely assume she was giving the guy a blowjob when he died."

The captain nodded and said, "That makes sense. What are you gonna do first?"

"I'm not sure yet," Brown said. "I was hoping you could come up with something," hoping to embarrass the captain in front of the new guy.

"Oh, yeah, right," the captain said musingly. "I'm supposed to be the genius in the house, right?"

"That's what they tell us," Brown said.

McKenzie stood there, smiling the entire time, watching the interplay between Brown and the captain as if it was a tennis match.

The captain looked up at him. "What do you think, McKenzie?"

Obviously, he didn't know what to do, and he was looking for McKenzie to help him out. McKenzie, on the other hand, didn't know what to say when faced with such a situation, and so he shook his head in wonder.

"That isn't the response I was expecting," the captain said.

"Well, captain," McKenzie said, "I wasn't expecting you to ask me such a thing. After all, I'm the new kid on the block."

"That's why I asked. In order for you to learn."

McKenzie shuffled his feet for a moment, then asked, "Interview her friends and associates?"

"Very good," the captain said. "Does that agree with you, Brown?"

"Sure," Brown said.

"Good," the captain said. "Now get outa here."

Brown led the way out of the captain's office, and went directly to his desk. McKenzie followed him and just stood there, waiting for Brown to acknowledge him.

Brown gestured to the desk across from him and said, "That's yours, McKenzie."

"Thanks," McKenzie said. "Should I bring my stuff over?"

"That's up to you."

"Thank you. I'll get my stuff."

McKenzie wandered away, and when he was out of sight, Brown went into the captain's office again.

The captain looked up. "What now?" he asked, aggrieved. "Look, Captain, I don't need that guy. I do best when I'm on my own."

"I know. You've told me that many times before. But you need backup, you need protection. Remember, this is a dangerous job."

"And I think it's going to be more dangerous with him around."

"That's your opinion, Brown. All McKenzie needs is to have his rough edges sanded off, and you are the one to do it. Understand?"

"So, I guess there's no further discussion, then."

"That's right. Now, get back to your desk before McKenzie comes back."

"Yes, sir," Brown said, standing at attention. He saluted, then turned on his heel and walked out.

When he got back to his desk, McKenzie was already at his, placing his possessions on top and around the desk and inside the drawers. Brown looked at him skeptically.

"You done?" he asked.

McKenzie looked up. "Yes, sir."

"Then let's get moving," and he stood up and walked out of the squad room, with McKenzie on his heels.

7

That night, Rowland met with the Borstrands again, this time in a shabby hotel somewhere in Harlem on 8th Avenue. They thought that the darkness would hide their pursuits. Rowland didn't really relish the idea of meeting at a hotel in the midst of all those you know what's. He wouldn't even say the n word to himself, a holdover from his days as a "liberal." He was no longer "liberal," and he was going to profess it to the world. His father had hated the blacks, and had been a member of the KKK. Rowland thought briefly about becoming a member, but that was too obvious and would surely come out to the public, and then he would definitely lose the black vote.

This time, Rowland didn't stop to look around; he already hated the place and didn't want to be there any longer than he had to. He rushed through the lobby to the elevators, but he had to wait because they were both being used. He stood in front of them looking straight ahead, again dressed in his Mets windbreaker and cap. An old black lady in shabby clothes walked up beside him and stared up at him. Rowland remained steadfast. The old lady lifted a hand and used it to caress Rowland's windbreaker.

Rowland gritted his teeth and kept looking straight ahead. Finally, the elevator on the left arrived and discharged a few lonely, decrepit figures, and Rowland entered quickly. The old lady followed him inside, and Rowland was forced to touch her to lead her out of the elevator.

He pressed the button for the fifth floor, and the elevator doors took an eternity to close. All the while, the old lady stared at him. He gritted his teeth some more until finally the doors closed. He let out a sigh of relief and watched the numbers above the door flash on and off until he reached the fifth floor. (Obviously, the Borstrands had a special something about the fifth floor, but for the life of him, he couldn't figure out what it was.) He stepped out of the elevator and looked around; he turned right until he reached 510. He knocked on the door and waited until Robert Borstrand opened the door and led him into the living room of the suite, where Julie was seated, waiting for his presence.

The usual amenities were exchanged, then they got down to business.

"So," Julie began, "how are you doing?"

"In what way?" Rowland asked.

"In the campaign way," she answered.

"Don't play hard to get, Eddie," Borstrand said.

"I'm not playing hard to get," Rowland insisted.

"Then tell us what's been going on."

Rowland hesitated, then said, "Did you see my news conference?"

"Oh, indeed we did," Borstrand said.

"What did you think of it?" Rowland asked.

Julie leaned forward. "You really want to know?" she asked.

"Sure."

"Well, then," Julie said, "here it is." She paused for a moment in order to collect her thoughts. "I think it had its moments, but it went too far. The bigotry behind the speech was hard to listen to. I didn't know you actually felt that way."

"I don't," Rowland lied. "It was an act. I meant it to be hard to listen to..."

"Except for those who believe in what you professed," Borstrand said.

"Yeah, well," Rowland said, "those people will remain in the shadows, because Julie will get elected. Isn't that the purpose of what we set out to do?"

Julie leaned forward. "You sort of took it too far, as far as I'm concerned. I just wanted you to present yourself as a candidate for president, not discuss any issues while doing so."

"But isn't that what I should do?" Rowland whined.

Borstrand stepped forward. "You're a fool, Eddie. You showed the public what a fool you are. Please try to pull back your vituperation. We don't want any sort of hateful rhetoric to overshadow the liberality of our purpose. Don't ruin this, Eddie. You're on the road to destroying our democracy."

"You really think so?" Rowland demanded. He stood up and faced Borstrand head-on. "Well, I think you're overreacting. I have no intention of destroying our democracy. I love this country. I wouldn't know what to do without it. I will defend this country with my life."

"Oh, really?" Borstrand asked. "You dodged the draft during the Vietnam War by claiming you had heel spurs."

"I do. You want to see?"

"What are you going to do? Cut open your heels and show them to us?"

"No. I can show you the X-rays."

"Wait. You still have the X-rays from the sixties?"

"I sure do. I'll go and get them now."

Julie decided it was time to stop this display of testosterone by saying, "Okay, gentlemen, it's time to cool down. Let's talk about this in a calm, reserved way."

Borstrand and Rowland seemed to go to their respective corners, while Julie took the reins of the conversation into her hands. "Now. Eddie, you've got this bigoted stance already set out, but we need you to pull back a little. Your main objective, as you well know, is to get rid of my competitors until there's nobody left but the two of us. You can't really do that if you're focused on the immigrant situation. You have to face it, Eddie, if we don't do something soon, this country will be in serious trouble."

Rowland shrugged. "What makes you think that?"

Julie smiled condescendingly and said, "You know, as well as I do, that a great many people in this country have hated the administration of Charles Grant..."

"Why?" Rowland interrupted, "because he's ... black?" He almost said the n-word, but stopped himself just in time.

"That's correct," Julie said. "You know, because you started the rumors that he wasn't born in the United States."

"I did not," Rowland said, in a huff.

"Oh, let's stop it, Eddie," Julie said. "Remember. Don't kid a kidder. I know all about it: how you wanted to destroy Charles' reputation, how you wanted to tear him down so you could build yourself up. These are dangerous times, Eddie, and you have to stop adding fuel to the fire."

Rowland began to sulk as he sat in a chair on the other side of the room.

"This is a great opportunity we're handing you, Eddie," Julie continued. "Just think, you can help us pull our republic together, to make democracy the most important part of our campaign. Without you, we might lose the country to bombastic figures, who want to rule the country as authoritarians. We can't afford to stoke the fires of hatred. We need to ensure that our country remains steadfast and that we have a firm hand on the controls. If we don't do that, this country will fall to the despots."

"Are you sure of that?" Rowland asked.

"Very sure, Eddie. Aren't we, Bobby?"

Borstrand had made himself a drink and was standing at the wet bar, leaning back against the wall. He stood up straight when his wife addressed him and said, "It's practically a done deal, Eddie. If we don't do something about the future, we'll be up shit's creek without a paddle. You've got to help us to secure the nomination, so that Julie can ride into the presidency on a white stallion, the heroine of the decade."

Rowland snickered. "That seems a little extreme, in my opinion."

"You know what I mean, Eddie. You need to cooperate, or I can assure you, we'll crush you."

"Is that a threat?" Rowland asked gutturally.

"As the kids say, Eddie, it's a promise."

Rowland seemed to growl in the back of his throat.

"Okay, gentlemen," Julie intervened, "enough of that." She turned to Rowland and practically pleaded with him. "We need your help, Eddie. You're the only one who can help us succeed."

By playing to his ego, Julie had scored a definite point.

Rowland's chest seemed to expand with every new breath he took. "You got a deal, babe," he said.

***

After the meeting with the Borstrands, Rowland found a quiet spot on the street where he could make a very private phone call. He dialed the number he knew by heart and spoke for a moment with Madame Pompidou. She had a soft, sultry, sexy voice, but Rowland didn't know if her face fit the voice, for he had never met her. All their transactions were done over the phone, and Rowland liked it that way. He had an account with her and therefore didn't need to give any information other than his name; he was certain that Madame Pompidou would not blackmail him, nor would anyone else in her organization.

When the arrangements were over, he took a cab to the hotel that was used for their assignations, a medium-grade hotel, with sheets changed after every meeting. He was pretty sure that the cabdriver did not recognize him because of his "disguise." He left the cab and walked into the hotel, where the man at the front desk nodded to him and then went back to reading his newspaper, a rarity in today's day and age, primarily because the man behind the desk was over seventy and liked the old ways; he was behind the times and didn't even own a cell phone; he was probably the last person in Manhattan to still have a landline.

Rowland was happy to breathe in the clean scent of his surroundings, instead of the grubbiness of the hotel he had just left. His meeting with the Borstrands had invigorated him; he now knew what he had to do. He would never have a meeting with the Borstrands again, and he would stick to the agenda that he and his cohorts had agreed upon. He was a nasty man, and he was turning his back on the Borstrands because he had grown away from their style of democracy. Oh, he would get rid of the competition, but only for his own sake, not for Julie's. His campaign would crush her until there was nothing left of her wimpy liberalism. He was determined now to rule this country with an iron fist, just like his hero, Adolf Hitler. No one else in his inner circle, or the world for that matter, knew that he worshipped Hitler. It was one of his many guilty pleasures, but he did not feel guilty of much of anything. He was a true sociopath, whose mania was infected by malignant narcissism. He thought he was perfectly healthy, while those around him knew better, and his supporters followed him because they believed in his bigoted, racist ethics.

Why did Rowland hide his indecent proclivities? Mainly because he was a public figure, and he didn't want the people of New York to hate him even more than they already did. He wasn't aware, however, that the majority of the people of New York didn't like him at all. He was oblivious to the true feelings of the New Yorkers around him. He thought he was loved by those who despised him. He was truly a person of his own making; he was not a self-made man, as he would have others think, because he was given a lot of money by his father, another real estate developer, a man from Germany who was as close to a Nazi as you could get without being in Berlin.

Rowland pretty much followed in his father's footsteps, but not until now was he able to express himself to his populace, for times had changed drastically. And not for the good.

Rowland knocked on the door of suite 318, and shortly, it was opened by a stunning brunette in lingerie. She displayed herself to him in all her glory.

"Well, good evening, Mr. Rowland," she said. "Won't you come in?"

Rowland smiled dreamily as he passed her, his hand brushing against her bare midriff, where he could feel the silky lusciousness of her bare skin. Even at his age, he felt his cock stir, and he was happy to see that his testosterone was still working.

The brunette closed the door behind him.

As she turned to him, he asked, "What's your name?"

"Anna," she said.

"That's a very simple name."

"The simpler, the better."

Rowland started to take off his clothes. "Wait a minute," Anna said.

He stopped what he was doing and looked at her quizzically.

"You usually ask for Litzy Baker," she told him. "Why me, all of a sudden?"

"Well, first of all," Rowland explained, "I didn't ask for you specifically. I gave Madame Pompidou a description of what I like, and she sent you. Is that okay?"

"Sure. But why didn't you just ask for Litzy?"

"Didn't you hear?" Rowland said solemnly. "She's dead. Murdered."

Anna gasped, and in the silence, a tear or two ran down her cheeks. "When?" she whispered.

"I don't know. But it wasn't too long ago."

"Do they know who did it?"

"Unfortunately, no. And I don't think they ever will."

"Why do you say that?"

"Because your johns are usually hard to find."

"How do you know it was one of her johns?"

"Just a guess. Now, can we get on with business?"

Anna went to bed and sat down. "I don't know if I can," she said breathlessly. "Not right now."

"You don't want my money?"

She looked up at him. "I thought you liked Litzy."

"I did. But she's gone and there's nothing I can do about it."

"You don't sound too broken up about it," Anna said defensively.

"Why should I be? She was a whore, and she's dead. You like simple? Well, it's as simple as that."

Anna shook her head. "What a horrible thing to say..."

"It's the truth."

"Is that the way you think about all of us?"

"You provide a service. A very nice one. I enjoy it immensely. But when it's over, you take my money and go on with your business. Am I supposed to feel sorry about that?"

"I see what you mean," Anna said. "What do you want done?"

"A blowjob. And I want you to swallow."

"You're a very cruel man," she said harshly.

"Do you want my money or not?"

She stood and said, "Get undressed."

As Anna worked on his cock, trying to make him get hard as best she could, he thought about what lay ahead. It was going to be a long, hard haul, but he was getting to the point where he believed he could actually win the presidency. He was forming a great team, that would push him to greater heights. He smiled, not at what Anna was doing but at the fact that at this time next year, he could be living in the White House.

His cock was having a hard time coming to life, but he really didn't care at the moment. He was just content to lie there, Anna's lips surrounding his flaccid member, and think about all the good stuff he could do when president. He would have to start slowly, of course, because he would want to get re-elected. He had to play it smart: just a taste of what he was really going to do. In his second term, he could do anything he wanted, simply because he would not be president anymore, he would be an autocratic leader of a country that would by then follow him to the ends of the earth. At least, enough of them to make a difference.

He was suddenly a very happy man, even though Anna was still having trouble arousing him, so he thought he'd help her out a little. He instructed her to turn herself around, so that her ass and pussy were in his face. He stuck his tongue up inside of her, while she continued her own permutations, and eventually he made her have an orgasm. But his cock remained at ease, so he got on his knees and told her to open her mouth. He took himself in his hand and jerked off until he squirted into her mouth, and without thinking about it, she swallowed all of his come. She even took the tip of his cock in her mouth and sucked him dry. He was a very happy and contented man now.

***

After Bobby Borstrand had shown Rowland out of the depressing suite of the depressing hotel, he returned to the living room, where he made drinks for he and his wife, and after the initial sip, he turned to her and asked, "Well, what do you think?"

"He's going to stab us in the back," Julie answered.

"I agree."

"He's going to seriously run for the presidency, and give me a very hard time during the campaign."

"Okay," Borstrand mused. "But why?"

"Very simple. He's an arrogant, disgusting pig, who only thinks about one thing: himself. I should never have approached him in the first place."

"Who else could you have asked?"

"I don't know," Julie said, with a shake of her head. "Maybe Ted Grossup..."

"Are you kidding? He never would have done it. He's too interested in running himself."

"Who isn't in this cockamamie world?" Julie said angrily.

"Calm down, my lady," Borstrand said, reassuringly. "We just have to watch out for the fucking bastard. These talks are doing no good. As far as I'm concerned, this should be the last time we meet with the prick."

"You're right," Julie said, calmly this time. "We made a mistake. We never should have thought about using him. He has never stood by his word, never once in his lifetime. Just like his father, another mean bastard."

"We just have to follow our campaign through to the end, and we're going to have to think of Rowland as just a minor annoyance. We can get rid of him, just like you would step on a cockroach." He took a few tentative steps toward the sofa where Julie sat, and stopped at the end opposite where she sat. "Now. Let's talk about us."

She looked up at him sharply. "What do you mean?"

"I want to talk about where we're going to go from here."

"You know the answer to that, Bobby. Grow up."

"I'm a grown-up. I just wonder about you sometimes.

She looked him in the eye and said, "Listen. This hasn't been a marriage for a very long time. Right now, it's just a convenience. We need to remain married if I plan to win the White House. Don't you understand that?"

"Oh, sure," Borstrand said, "I understand. But I don't think you understand."

"How's that?"

"I was once president. Now, you expect me to be First Gentleman. Isn't that a step down?"

"No, I don't think so. By being First Gentleman, you make history."

"I don't want to make any more history. I've already made history..."

"Yes," she snapped, "for getting a blow-job in the oval office."

"That's not what I mean," Borstand said, containing his anger.

"Then what do you mean?"

He paused significantly before saying, "I still love you, Julie..."

"You have a strange way of showing it," she replied.

"Maybe so," he conceded, "but I want us to be closer than we have been for the past twenty years."

"That's not going to happen," she said coldly. "As the old expression goes, you've made your bed..."

"And now I have to lie in it," Borstrand interrupted, "but I don't have to like it."

"That's none of my concern. You thought you could play around on me without there being any consequences. Well, now you see you've been wrong."

"I admit that. But can't you forgive me?"

She glared at him. "No," she said simply.

"Why the hell not?"

"How dare you? How dare you pretend to be the victim in this? You've broken my heart time and time again. I've looked the other way because I didn't want to end our marriage. I stayed with you because I wanted to be First Lady. And now I want to be president. And I want you next to me because you have been so popular in the past. As a matter of fact, you're still very popular, for reasons I truly cannot understand. But at your name, there are people who practically come to attention. You have earned the respect of some, and the hatred of others. But your name brings back a lot of good memories, and you are asked time and time again to make speeches to ladies' clubs and the American Legion and other right-wing organizations, even though you've been a die-hard liberal for most of your life. And now you have the audacity to question why I don't want to play wife anymore. You should be ashamed of yourself."

She stood up and walked away from him. He took another few

tentative steps and stood just five feet away from her. Her back was to him, but he didn't seem to mind.

"Please, Julie," he implored, "give me another chance."

She turned to him and said, "You're only saying this because you're way too old to get some young thing to suck you off."

"Do you have to be so vulgar?"

"It's what you've made me, Bobby. I'm not the young babe you met in college anymore. I'm a mature woman, who has become disgusted by the way she's been treated. You're responsible for all that. You call me vulgar. Well, you're crass, my loving husband. I know what you want from me: the occasional hand-job. Well, I'm not prepared to give it to you anymore, and I'm certainly not prepared to give you a blowjob anymore. You'll have to go to one of your fancy hookers to get that type of satisfaction. And I know you do. Occasionally, that is. Just leave me alone for now. We'll see how smoothly the campaign runs, then we'll talk about it after the election." She turned to face him. "Deal?"

"Yes, ma'am."

"Good. Now, leave, please. I intend to sleep here tonight."

"You did that the last time, too," he protested.

"I prefer being alone for the night."

She stared him down, and after a while, he turned away from her and shamefacedly left the suite, closing the door softly behind him.

8

That same night, Brown and his new partner arrived at the door of Litzy Baker's neighbor, Nancy Evans. They had called ahead and were expected. Nancy stood on the threshold of her door when they came up the stairs. She was dressed in jeans and a baggy pullover. She smiled at them and they followed her inside her apartment to the living room, a small, neat room, adequately furnished with a loveseat and two armchairs across a coffee table. Brown and his partner sat in the armchairs. Nancy asked if she could get them something to drink, but they declined courteously.

"Now," Brown began, "just some follow-up questions, if you don't mind."

"No, of course not," Nancy said, "anything I can do to help."

"Thank you. But before we begin, I need your full name."

"Certainly. It's Nancy Evans," and she spelled her last name, even though there was really no need to.

"Thank you, Ms. Evans. I realize that you might not have gotten over what happened by now, but we need to question you while everything is still fresh in your mind."

"I understand completely."

McKenzie leaned forward and said, "I'm sorry for your loss, ma'am."

"Thank you, detective, but she wasn't a relative of mine. Just a friend."

"Still..."

"Thank you very much."

After this exchange, she sat there primly, waiting for the questioning to begin. At first, Brown did his best to try to not glare at his partner, but he found himself unable to do so. So, he pulled his focus away from McKenzie and onto Nancy.

"Okay, Ms. Evans," he began. "Tell me about the last time you saw Ms. Baker."

"I saw her the other night. I went over to her place and we arranged a weekend at some spa I had passes for. At first, she was reluctant to go, but then she got excited about it. We were going to have a good time."

"I'm sure you were," Brown said. "Now, the last time I talked to you, you mentioned something about Eddie Rowland."

McKenzie's eyes opened wide, and he looked closely at Nancy.

"Well," she started slowly, "I guess you already know that Litzy was a ... prostitute..."

Brown nodded. McKenzie kept his eyes on Nancy.

"Well," she began again, her shyness evaporating suddenly, "she told me about her johns, and one of them was Eddie Rowland. He was a big pain in the neck, but he spent a lot of money on her. I mean, a lot of money. That's the only reason she catered to him. Otherwise, she had nothing good to say about him."

"What did she say in particular?" Brown asked.

"She said he was a fat pig..." She stopped immediately and began to blush. "I'm sorry about the expression, but it was hers. I don't use such expressions when talking about someone, even when I don't like that someone. Frankly, she was disgusted by him and wished she didn't have to deal with him, but as I said, he paid well."

Brown asked, "Was she afraid of him?"

She shook her head and said, "I don't understand the question," hesitantly.

"Did he ever threaten her?" McKenzie asked suddenly.

Brown couldn't hide his glare this time.

"No," Nancy said softly, "not that I know of."

"So, she didn't tell you about anything like that?" Brown jumped in before McKenzie had a chance.

"I don't remember anything like that," Nancy said softly

"Okay," Brown said. "Now, were any of her other johns famous?"

"Not that I know of. At least, she didn't tell me about anybody else."

"You mean, she didn't mention other johns?"

"I'm sorry. She mentioned other johns, but not by name."

"So, from what you understood, Ms. Baker didn't have any other celebrities on her list?"

"List?" Nancy asked, obviously confused.

"Her list of johns."

"They keep lists?"

"I believe so," Brown conceded.

"Well, she didn't mention anybody else by name."

"Could it be she didn't mention them because she thought you might not have heard of them?"

She took offense. "Do you think I'm some kind of a hick?"

"Well," Brown said, "I must admit you don't sound like a New Yorker."

"All right, I'm from Ohio, but that doesn't mean I don't hear things or read things…"

"I understand, Ms. Evans, but there are certain personalities in this city that other people around the country have never heard of."

"Well, I've been living here for five years now. I assure you, I'm up on my New York celebrities."

McKenzie broke in. "Detective Brown didn't mean to upset you, Ms. Evans. He just needs to ask certain questions in order to try to discover who killed Ms. Baker…"

"I don't need you to defend me," Brown reprimanded him, sharply.

McKenzie seemed to shrink into himself; he didn't say anything for the rest of the interview.

Brown asked some more questions of Nancy, but she didn't seem to have any more information to give him. Any strange men hanging around? Any mysterious phone calls? Did she ask for any kind of help? What was her state of mind the last time they spoke together? Did she seem satisfied with her life? How was she as a neighbor? As a friend? What did she do in her personal life? Did she ever see Rowland outside of work?

Nancy's answers to these questions were not very satisfying, but Brown kept on asking them, while McKenzie sat idly by and pouted. At last, Brown stood up to leave, and McKenzie followed suit. Nancy led them to the door and showed them out. Brown said if he had any more questions, he'd get in touch, and he handed her his card, saying if she thought of anything, however minor, she should call him. Nancy smiled and shut the door quietly behind them. Brown took the stairs down, and McKenzie followed, still not saying anything.

When they were in the car with Brown driving, Brown looked briefly at McKenzie and asked, "What's your problem?"

McKenzie remained steadfast. "Nothing. Never mind."

Brown drove silently for a while, then said, "Look, if I said anything back there that upset you, I didn't mean to. We're new together, so I don't know if I can trust you. Just show me who you are, and if I like it, we'll be partners. Otherwise, if we're in an interview, wait for me to look at you before you ask a question. Understood?"

McKenzie shrugged. "Yes, sir," he said solemnly.

Brown looked over at him once more, then turned his head forward and drove silently into the night.

9

Mike Espinoza was on his appointed rounds: he was following the campaign trail of Edward "Eddie" Rowland as they swept through the heartland of America, where everyone they met seemed, for some reason, to adore him. Mike shook his head every time a voter would come up to Rowland and shake his hand, and some women would even kiss it, as if he was the pope. Rowland smiled and accepted their obeisance as if it was his due.

Mike wrote his reports on his laptop, which he always carried with him when on these trips, and sent them to the paper, who published them the same day. Mike just reported the news, he did not elaborate on it with his personal views. Rowland had taken notice of him shortly after he started reporting, and he admired Mike for the reticence he showed. Other reporters were tearing Rowland apart, but Mike just reported on what was happening, not on what he felt or thought.

Personally, Mike despised Rowland for what he considered was the raping of New York City. Rowland bought up properties, renovated them without paying his contractors for their work, and then wouldn't rent or sell to any black people, no matter how much they made, nor how much their portfolio showed that they were wealthy. Rowland was an out-and-out bigot, just the same as his father, who had admired the Nazi party during WWII and remained an anti-Semite for most of his life.

Rowland couldn't say he was an anti-Semite out loud, because his daughter, Priscilla, had married a Jew, something he found very hard to stomach. But he welcomed him into the family because Priscilla obviously cared for him, and because his son-in- law was as far from being a real Jew as anyone he knew. He was not a practicing Jew, nor did he dress like one in the eyes of the bigoted Rowland. The son of a bitch was a Gentile through and through, in his manner and the way he talked, and Rowland, if elected, would make him ambassador to Israel in order to bring peace in the Middle East. Or at least that's what he thought. He had even started thinking about actually becoming president. He was seriously deluded, but the people who came up to him on the campaign trail showed him an obedience that couldn't be swayed.

Mike didn't know this at the time, but he would soon find out, and then his reporting would become biased, but very subtly; he would not do anything to visibly upset Rowland, who wouldn't understand any of it because he had the vocabulary of a 3rd grader, and the mentality of a true idiot. While Rowland spoke at one of his rallies, Mike worked on his laptop, furiously writing every word said. Mike could type 120 wpm, so his speed kept him well above the fray. None of his colleagues could match him, and he flew above the riffraff with a tenacity that thrilled his bosses.

Rowland gave one of his smug smiles to the crowd who adored him. If only they knew, Mike thought. As Rowland worked the crowd like the buffoon he was, Mike was frozen in place when he thought of the danger Rowland presented to the country. The problem was that most of Rowland's supporters were buffoons as well, and they thought Rowland's actions and speech were reflective of their own concerns. However, the Democrats were doing no better, mainly because their party seemed to be strictly for the elite, not for the poor, especially poor-white trash.

The Democrats had to change their plans, or else they would be in the doghouse.

After the rally was over, Mike was packing up his things, when one of Rowland's aides came up to him to inform him that Mr. Rowland wanted to see him. Mr.? Mike thought. What a joke. But instead of speaking out loud, he threw his backpack over his shoulder and followed the anonymous figure backstage, where Rowland was smiling broadly at his supporters who were coming up to him to shake his hand, and possibly kiss his ring.

Mike felt nauseous.

After the last supporter was gone, Rowland came over to Mike with his hand outstretched. Mike reluctantly took it.

"Mr. Espinoza," Rowland said enthusiastically, "welcome, welcome. It's a great pleasure to meet you." He smiled more broadly. "I've been reading your articles."

Mike had to smile at that, not because he was pleased, but because he knew for a fact that Rowland didn't read anything. In fact, everything he wanted to look at was read to him by someone else. He's such a fraud, Mike thought.

"I've been very impressed," Rowland continued. "How'd you like to work for me?"

Mike was stunned, and it took him a few seconds to get out his words. "I'm flattered, Mr. Rowland, but I already have a job."

"I'll triple your salary. You can't beat that offer."

"But what do I tell my boss?"

"Tell him you're going to work for the next president of the United States."

Mike had to smile at that, also. An idea was percolating inside of his brain, an idea that might just win him a Pulitzer.

"Can I think it over?" he asked Rowland.

"Sure," Rowland said, "just don't take too much time. I'm a busy man."

Mike smiled again before saying, "You'll get my answer tomorrow."

They shook on it, then Rowland turned and walked away without saying anything else, as if the conversation had never taken place.

Mike left the venue and hurried to his hotel.

Mike got to his hotel room, where he quickly prepared his laptop for a video call. When he was done, he called the editor-in-chief of the newspaper, Terry Wainwright. It took a while, but Wainwright finally came on the line.

"What's up, cub reporter?" he asked, with a contemptuous sneer in his voice.

"Hey, boss," Mike greeted him, "you won't believe what just happened."

"Amaze me."

"Rowland wants to hire me."

Wainwright became alert. "Really?" he asked. "What does he want you to do?"

"Write his speeches, I guess."

"Well, that should be good. Then he won't sound like an eight-year-old."

"So, you think it's a good idea?" Mike asked.

"Of course I don't think it's a good idea," Wainwright snapped. "We've been a Democratic newspaper since the beginning. You can't switch camps like that."

"Why not?"

Wainwright paused. "You mean, you're seriously considering it?" he asked seriously.

"Yes," Mike answered, "but not in the way you think."

There was a silence while Wainwright considered this. "Go on," he said.

"If I accept Rowland's offer," Mike began, "I could go undercover. While I'm writing his speeches, if that's what he wants me to do, I could also be writing a series of articles from the inside. Get me? I could be a spy for the newspaper."

A semblance of a smile appeared on Wainwright's lips. "You think you can pull it off?" he asked admiringly.

"I'm sure of it. The only thing is, we need to make it look good. You've got to start spreading the word that I quit to go work for Rowland, and you're pissed as hell. As you've said, we've always been a Democratic newspaper, and now I've gone over to the other side for a bundle of money."

"I'm sure it will be," Wainwright affirmed, "but you need to go all the way. You need to convince Rowland that you've changed sides. You need to be very convincing."

"I will be," Mike said, "don't worry about it."

"When do you want to start?"

"I told him I'd give him my answer tomorrow."

"That soon, huh?"

"Why not?" Mike asked. "The sooner, the better."

Wainwright shrugged. "All right. It's your funeral."

"Please don't put it that way."

Part III:
The End

1

Detective Ted Brown was at his desk one morning, when he received a visitor. It was the wife of Earl Lester, the corpse with a perpetual erection. It still hadn't gone down, and Mrs. Lester was very peeved by this, for she couldn't have an open casket at his funeral; it would be obscene.

"I understand your predicament," Brown said to her, "but what can I do about it?"

"Find the person who murdered him," she insisted.

"He wasn't murdered, Mrs. Lester, he died of natural causes."

"I saw that on the death certificate, but I don't believe it. After all, why is he ... the way ... he is?"

She obviously found this conversation embarrassing.

Brown was trying his best to console her. "Listen, Mrs. Lester, we have some leads that I can't tell you about, but when I get to the bottom of things, I'll let you know."

"Look, you're a very nice young man, and I know what a hard job you have, but what do I tell my friends and family?"

"I wish I could help you there, ma'am, but that's beyond my pay grade."

He smiled reassuringly, but, unfortunately, she was not reassured. She stood up and said, "I'll be expecting to hear from you in a couple of weeks. If I don't, I can assure the commissioner will hear all about it," and she trounced out of the room, with her head held high.

Brown chuckled to himself.

His new partner, McKenzie, stepped forward and said, "That was pretty slick, Ted."

Brown looked up in surprise. "What?"

"The way you handled that lady, but aren't you worried about her contacting the commissioner?"

"If I had a dime for every time I've been threatened by a civilian, I'd truly be a millionaire."

"Not even a billionaire?"

Brown shook his head. "I said a dime," and he smiled, the first time he had ever smiled at McKenzie, a good sign that tensions were beginning to ease.

McKenzie said, "So? What do we do now?"

Brown thought a minute, then said, "I'd like you to run a background check on Litzy Baker."

"The victim?"

"That's right."

"But isn't that a little unorthodox?"

"Sure is. But I think it might lead us somewhere."

"I'm on it," McKenzie said, and instantly retreated to his desk.

Brown smiled to himself and then went back to his own work.

***

Around 45 minutes later, McKenzie returned to Brown's desk with a sheaf of papers in his hand. "She was quite something, that girl," he said.

"What do you mean?" Brown asked.

"Read for yourself," McKenzie said, and handed him the papers.

Brown looked at them first, noticing the size of the sheaf, and then

167

looked up at McKenzie, who had a small smile of triumph on his face. Brown started reading.

Finally, Brown looked up. "It says here she was a Rhodes Scholar."

"That's right," McKenzie confirmed.

"Then why was she working as a hooker?"

"The correct term is sex worker."

"Whatever."

"I don't know," McKenzie said, with a shrug. "Maybe she liked having sex."

"She could have sex in her private life. Why did she have to use it as a profession?"

McKenzie shrugged again. "You got me."

Brown continued reading. "She graduated with honors from every school she went to."

"That's right."

"Then why was she a whore?"

"A sex worker."

"Whatever."

"Listen, Ted," McKenzie said, leaning toward him, "there's something very strange about this woman's background. We need to ask some more questions."

Brown read on. He came to a paragraph that recounted the meeting Litzy had had with Rowland, who came to her school to give the commencement address. Curiouser and curiouser, Brown thought, even though he had never read Alice in Wonderful or Through the Looking Glass. Brown was not much of a reader; in fact, he didn't even like reading the papers McKenzie had given him to read. He also didn't like writing reports, but then again, that was a necessary evil, something he'd learned to tolerate in order to keep his job.

But now, he doesn't know what to make of the information given to him by McKenzie. He looked up at his young partner and grinned. "I think we need to ask some more questions," he affirmed.

McKenzie nodded and said, "I think we do, too, partner. You ready to go?"

Brown was finally having fun. "You bet," he said, grabbed his coat, and headed for the door, with McKenzie on his heels.

***

Al Hanson stood by the window of Rowland's office in Manhattan and stared out upon the wonders of the city. He was sure that one time soon, Rowland would be president and use his new republicanism to run this country with an iron hand. The authoritarianism that existed within Rowland needed to come out, and he was the man to do it. Rowland was a fucking moron, as most people who knew him would agree, but he was a lump of clay able to be molded, and he was the sculptor who could mold him into shape.

The phone on Rowland's desk gave a sharp beep-beep! And Hanson went to the desk and picked it up. "Yes? ... Who? ... Did you tell them that Mr. Rowland was out of town? ... Uh-huh ... Uh-huh ... I see. Tell them if they want to meet with me, I'll be happy to accommodate them," and then he hung up the phone and waited for the door to open. He did not sit behind Rowland's desk.

Shortly, the door opened and Miss Stanhope, certainly a blonde bombshell if there ever was one, stepped in, followed by Detectives Brown and McKenzie, who were not at all deferential, but should they have been? Hanson wasn't sure; after all, he wasn't the man the detectives wanted to speak with. Hanson stepped forward to greet them.

"Hello, gentlemen," he said exuberantly, "welcome, welcome!"

"Thank you, sir," Brown said, "I'm Detective Brown, and this is Detective McKenzie. Who do we have the pleasure of speaking to?"

"Albert Hanson, best friend of Mr.Rowland's," he said, then turned to Miss Stanhope, who was still standing in the doorway. "Please bring us some coffee, Miss Stanhope."

"Certainly, sir," Miss Stanhope said, and turned and wiggled her magnificent ass as she closed the door behind her. However, the detectives were not impressed, for they stayed focused on Hanson and no one else.

"Please," Hanson said, "have a seat."

There was a couch by the wall facing the window, and the detectives decided to use that to park their less than magnificent asses. Hanson parked his in the armchair across the coffee table from them.

"I'm sorry, gentlemen," he said, "but Mr. Rowland is out of town, on the campaign trail."

"Thank you, Mr. Hanson," Brown said, "his secretary gave us the news."

"Then why would you want to see me?" Hanson asked.

"You answered that question already, Mr. Hanson," Brown said. "You told us you're Mr. Rowland's best friend."

"That's right," Hanson said, "I am. But you couldn't have known that before you came in."

"Oh, but I did, Mr. Hanson," McKenzie chimed in. "You see, I do a lot of reading when I'm working, and part of my reading material are newspapers. There was an article not too long ago about you, and I happened to read it."

Brown smiled smugly.

"I see," Hanson said.

The door to the office opened suddenly, and Miss Stanhope came back in, carrying a tray with a coffee pot on it, and three cups and saucers. She moved gracefully to the coffee table and laid the tray in front of the men gathered around it.

"Thank you, Miss Stanhope," Hanson said. "That will be all."

She smiled at them, and as she retreated through the door, she gave her ass one long wiggle before closing the door behind her.

"Nice young lady," Hanson said approvingly. "Good secretary."

"I'm sure," McKenzie said, forcing his eyes from the door she had disappeared through.

"Coffee, gentlemen?" Hanson asked as he leaned forward to pour.

"Not for me, thanks," Brown said.

"I'll have a cup," McKenzie said.

Hanson poured for both of them, and McKenzie put some cream and sugar into his cup and stirred it slowly.

Hanson got comfortable in his chair and said, "Well, gentlemen, what can I do for you?"

It had taken a while, but he finally got to the point.

Brown looked closely at him and asked, "How much do you know about Rowland's private life?"

Hanson gave a start. "Is that relevant to what you are investigating?" he asked.

"It might be."

"By the way," Hanson said, "what is it you are investigating?"

"We're looking into the death of a woman by the name of Litzy Baker."

"Who's she?"

"You've never heard of her?"

"No."

"Mr. Rowland's never mentioned her?"

"No."

Brown looked at McKenzie, who took over the questioning.

"How about Earl Lester?" McKenzie asked. "Ever hear of him?"

"No," Hanson said, with a slight shrug of his shoulders.

There was a slight pause, then Brown asked, "What does Mr. Rowland do in his leisure time?"

Hanson answered, "He watches television."

"What exactly?"

"The news."

"What station?"

"Fox News, but I don't see what that has anything to do with."

"I'm just curious," Brown responded.

"Does that mean you're going to vote for Mr. Rowland?" Hanson asked expectantly.

"I don't think so," Brown said slowly.

"Why not?"

Brown stared at him. "Look at my skin color, Mr. Hanson."

"What about it?"

"It's the wrong color."

"I beg your pardon?"

"Mr. Rowland doesn't like black people."

"Who says so?"

"Nobody has to say anything," Brown said. "All they have to do is look at his history."

Hanson sat up straight. "Why did you come here?" he said in a rough voice.

"I came here to see a bunch of downright hypocrites."

"Cool it, Ted," McKenzie warned.

"There's a woman lying in the morgue right now who seemed to know Rowland very well," Brown said levelly.

"So?" Hanson inquired. "Mr. Rowland knows a lot of people."

"Does he know a dead woman named Litzy Baker?"

"I don't know."

"She was a prostitute."

"Mr. Rowland does not deal with prostitutes. In fact, he was one of the members of the committee to clean up the streets of New York."

"That's a lie, and you know it."

"Come on, Ted," McKenzie said, "let's get outa here."

He took Brown's arm, and Brown shook him off. "Not just yet," he said.

Hanson stood up. "Shall I call security?"

Brown laughed in his face. "Try it."

Hanson moved to the desk and picked up the phone. After a moment, he said, "Miss Stanhope, call security right away. That's right. Right away!" he screamed into the transmitter, then slammed the phone down.

Brown smiled. "Why are you losing your cool, Mr. Hanson? Do you know something I should know?"

"Get out," Hanson growled.

It was at that moment that two brawny security men in black suits came through the door.

"That's okay," Brown said, holding out his hands. "We're leaving."

Hanson fumed silently.

Brown moved toward the door and said, "If we have any more questions, we'll be back," over his shoulder. He went out the office door, followed closely by McKenzie.

***

When they got back into their car, McKenzie asked Brown, "So did we learn anything?"

"We sure did," Brown said.

"What's that?"

"He lied his ass off," Brown said. "They sure have something to hide."

He put the car in gear and they drove off.

***

When Hanson was finally alone, he took out his handkerchief and wiped his palms; they had been sweating since the beginning of the interrogation. Or was it really an interrogation? Or just a fishing expedition? After all, almost everybody knew that term from the TV show Law and Order, so Hanson was well-up on the jargon that was used nowadays.

After a moment's thought, Hanson sat behind Rowland's desk and pressed a button on the telephone console. When Miss Stanhope answered, quite surprised by the fact that Mr. Hanson was using Mr. Rowland's phone, Hanson asked her to get in touch with Mr. Rowland as soon as possible. She said she would, and disconnected the call.

Hanson sat back in Rowland's desk chair and admired how comfortable it was. But his comfortability was soon interrupted by the burr of the telephone. He picked it up and was told by Miss Stanhope that Rowland was not available at the moment, but he would call back as soon as he was free. Hanson thanked her and hung up the phone, quite disturbed. If things continued as they were bound to, Rowland would not win the election, and Hanson would be set adrift. He didn't like the thought at all.

At almost two hours, the phone rang again, and Hanson picked it up, having not moved at all for the length of time he waited. When he put the phone to his ear, Miss Stanhope told him that Mr. Rowland was on the line; she transferred the call, and soon Rowland was yelling in his ear: "What's up, Al?"

"I was just talking with two detectives from the NYPD," Hanson informed him.

"What'd they want?"

"To talk to you."

"About what?" Rowland asked impatiently, his voice almost a scream.

"Calm down, Eddie. You must have had one hell of a rally."

"It was great. Fantastic. They loved me."

"Let's hope it stays that way."

"What's that supposed to mean?"

"The detectives are investigating a death," Hanson stated flatly.

"Oh, yeah? Who died?"

"A woman named Litzy Baker."

Suddenly, there was a deep silence.

"Are you still there, Eddie?"

"Yeah," Rowland said, softly and slowly, "I'm still here."

"You know her?"

Another silence.

"Eddie?"

"Yeah?"

"Well?"

"Yeah, I know her," Rowland said.

Hanson lost his temper. "Don't be so nonchalant about it, Eddie. You shouldn't get mixed up in the death of some young lady if you're going to win the presidency."

"What's it got to do with me?" Rowland asked, aggrieved.

"Everything. Your entire reputation."

There was a short pause.

"Why are they investigating?"

"Obviously, there's something suspicious about it. And you've got to keep yourself separate from it if you expect to win the White House."

"The way things are lookin' now, I'm a shoo in."

"It's never that simple."

"Then what do I do?"

"Get ahead of this."

"How?"

"By calling the cops," Hanson explained.

"I'll be glad to," Rowland said. "Just give me their number."

"Gladly," Hanson said, and he read off the names and numbers from the card Brown had left behind. "Got it?"

"Sure, Al. I'm not an idiot, you know."

"Sometimes you act like one."

That gave Rowland pause, and they talked for a few minutes more, Rowland trying his best to prove to Hanson that he wasn't an idiot. When they finally hung up, Hanson took a flask from his coat pocket and downed a large swig. Fine Scotch whiskey. He certainly needed it. But it didn't do any good, for Hanson had a lot on his plate, and he was especially worried about a cop case that might include his buddy's presidential bid. For one thing, Rowland could lose because he wasn't taking it seriously enough; for another, he could lose because he was a total schmuck. Hanson took another swig from his flask, but in spite of the warmth that traveled down his esophagus into his stomach, after having talked with Rowland, he was becoming a nervous wreck.

2

Mike Espinoza was leaning back in his chair, sipping a glass of very fine Scotch whiskey, watching Rowland as he talked about himself continuously. Rowland stood at the window of the hotel in Cleveland, where they were staying as a part of his campaign.

Tonight, there would be another one of his rallies, which would be covered favorably by Mike, who would then write unfavorably of him to his undercover editor.

This had been going on for some time now. The articles favoring Rowland were published in one of the sleazier newspapers, a tabloid from way back, while the unfavorable ones were growing enormously as the editor of The New York Herald Tribune was storing them in a secret room, where they would be kept until the time to put them into journalistic print. The editor, Terry Wainwright, thought Mike had done a brilliant job of uncovering some of Rowland's nastier habits; when the articles were finally published, they would put Rowland out of running for the presidency.

At this moment, Rowland was expounding upon his experiences when he was a young man, first getting into real estate as proscribed by his father, a man of inestimable wealth, who was a bigoted, racist, Nazi-era repeat. Rowland had loved his father and followed in his footsteps when it came to his attitude toward blacks, Jews, and just anybody who wasn't White Anglo-Saxon Protestant. Rowland truly believed that he was an ancestor of Pilgrims who had landed at Plymouth Rock and did their best—after a while—to rid the New Land of the inhabitants who were already there: friendly Indians who wanted to live in peace with their neighbors. Unfortunately, their new neighbors were evil, degenerate newcomers who wanted all the land for themselves and, therefore, needed to do away with the Redskins, as they called them. And we celebrate the massacre of these people every November, an irony in itself. Rowland was proud of his "ancestors" and their atavistic moods; he sometimes wished he had been one of them.

Mike sipped his whiskey as he thought about other things while Rowland spoke incessantly, something he did throughout his rallies, never sticking to the point, always admiring himself in practically every word he spoke. Rowland had already been diagnosed as a malignant narcissist; Mike could see that in everything he did. He had found enough dirt on Rowland to keep him from becoming president, but he wanted more, as much as he could gather to destroy whatever reputation Rowland had at the moment. The whiskey was great, the tirade not so much.

Finally, Rowland stopped talking and asked Mike, "Why aren't you taking any notes?"

Mike looked up suddenly and said, "I didn't know I was supposed to."

"Of course you're supposed to," Rowland insisted. "I'm telling you the story of my life. I want you to write it down."

"Why?"

"To make it a book."

Mike's eyes opened wide as he choked on his whiskey. "What?"

"You heard me. I want you to write my autobiography."

"You mean biography," Mike corrected him gently, because Rowland was not someone who liked to be corrected.

"No," Rowland said firmly, "autobiography."

Mike waited a moment before saying, "You mean, you want me to ghost-write your autobiography?"

"If that's what it takes to get it published, yeah."

"You want to publish your autobiography?"

"That's right," Rowland said smugly.

"Shouldn't you then write it yourself?"

"Why should I do it, when I have you?"

Mike had to think that one over for a minute. He was aware that Rowland had the vocabulary of a 3rd grader, and probably couldn't write any better. So, it seemed that Mike would have to do the hard work, while Rowland would reap all the glory. However, Mike might get some juicy tidbits that he could hammer into shape for his own articles. It was a win-win situation in Mike's eyes. As soon as he could manage it, he would call his editor and announce the good news. Wainwright would be so pleased.

Mike finished his whiskey and said, "It's a deal, big guy." He stood up and headed for the door.

Rowland asked, "Where are you going?"

"It's late and I've got to get some sleep before we embark on this new endeavor."

"See? Those are the kind of words I need in my book."

His book? Mike thought. It's already his book? Well, he's the one footing the bill, so why shouldn't he call it his book before they've even started on it?

Mike smiled and said, "Those are the only kind of words I know."

"Great," Rowland said exuberantly. He moved to Mike and slapped him on the back. "You'll see. This partnership of ours will blossom into true literature."

"You think so?"

"I know so."

Yeah, right, Mike thought, what he knows about literature could fit in a thimble.

"Well," Mike said, "I have no doubt you're right. Good night."

He opened the door, but Rowland put his hand out and closed it. "You really think this is a great idea?"

"Sure, Eddie, sure. It'll be the perfect lead-up to your campaign."

"Do you think we can get it out there so fast?"

"With me behind it, we'll have it out in no time."

Mike quickly opened the door and slipped out, before Rowland could make another move to delay him. When he got to his hotel room, he stripped and took a hot shower to get the grime of Rowland's personality off him. Lately, he'd been taking a great number of showers.

***

The next few days were a flurry of excitement and work, for Mike was finally in his element. He listened to Rowland talk about himself, but then Rowland would even get bored with that and walk out of the room without saying a word. Mike had already known that Rowland had the attention span of a gnat, but it was proven over and over again by his actions.

So, Mike labored on, using the bits and pieces of Rowland's life to form a tapestry of a man who really didn't care about anyone but himself. And that included his family. Very rarely did Rowland talk about his children, or his ex-wives, or his many business deals that went bust and those that were successful. When he did talk, he bragged about himself at an exceptionally high level, being sure to tap into his many successful liaisons with women he hardly knew. He considered himself a Lothario of the highest order, a man who women swooned over when he touched them, or spoke to them.

When Mike was finished for the day, he stood up and stretched. Tonight was a night off. No rallies; no bull sessions with Rowland. He was on his own, and thank goodness for that. He had the night to himself. What was he going to do? Find a nice bar somewhere and get slowly but surely drunk? Go to a movie? Find a young boy somewhere and fuck his brains out? No, not that. He was committed to his partner, and he had no intention of breaking the silent vows they might have said to one another.

At first, Mike thought about staying in for the night, calling room service and having his meal delivered, so he could stay in his room and watch TV while eating. Sounded like a plan. But then he thought he's in Utah now—Salt Lake City, to be exact—and he has the night off, so why not explore the city? That's a better plan. He put his coat on and headed for the lobby, but as he started to go through the revolving doors to the street, he stopped suddenly, blocking a couple trying to get to the street themselves, and thought about what kind of sights could be distinguished in Salt Lake City: maybe the Tabernacle for the truly religious citizens of the city.

But when he thought of possibly seeing Mitt Romney, his stomach turned over, and he finally responded to the insistent pushing of the people behind him by continuing into a complete revolution until he was back in the lobby again. The young couple behind him were finally released onto the street, and the young man subtly gave Mike the finger, which made Mike smile. If this were New York, he would probably go after the guy and get into a fight. He shook his head. No, he wouldn't; he was a lover, not a fighter. A pacifist.

So, he looked around and saw that there was a bar off in the far corner. He went in that direction and found the place rather busy for a Tuesday night. Then again, what did he know about the night life of Utah? Not very much. All he knew was that it was settled by the Mormons. That's really all he wanted to know anyway. So, he sidled up to the bar where there was a lone stool and took possession of it. He started out slowly by ordering a non-alcoholic beer. He didn't want to get drunk so quickly. When it arrived, he sipped it while looking around him covertly. He didn't want anyone to know he was on the prowl. Not that he was up to no good. Of course not. He just wanted to find someone or something that might entertain him for the rest of the night. After a long moment, he found someone he recognized: Arthur Lund, one of Rowland's closest bodyguards. What was he doing here? Mike wondered. Shouldn't he be upstairs outside Rowland's hotel door? But then again, Mike continued to think, maybe one of the other bodyguards was on duty. Lund was drinking a martini, it looked like, and trying to seduce a young and impressionable woman. Instead of her falling into his lap, she was resisting his every move, trying very hard to restrain him from raping her right then and there.

The night wore on, with Lund consuming more martinis and getting drunker by the minute; with the girl trying very hard to escape the clutches of the man who expected every woman to spread her legs for him at a moment's notice; and with Mike sitting by himself, drinking his beer slowly, and watching Lund as closely as he could without Lund noticing. Lund's back was to him, so the idea of him turning around suddenly and spotting Mike was unimaginable. After all, Lund was too wrapped up in the young woman who was turning away from him as much as possible without making it too obvious that she was planning her escape, all the while.

At close to midnight, when the bar was getting ready to close, a call came through on Lund's phone. He pulled the phone out of his pocket, glanced at the name on the screen, and almost instantly became sober. He lifted the phone to his ear, listened for a second, then made some excuse to the young lady who was with him (she almost let out a sigh of relief in his face), and stood up, staggering just slightly, to leave the bar. Mike watched this pantomime with some interest—after all, he'd only had two non-alcoholic beers—and after letting Lund go for a minute or two, he stood up and crossed to the lobby, where he saw Lund getting into an elevator. Mike watched the display above the elevator, and saw that it stopped at the 3rd floor, the floor where Rowland was staying. He hurried to the elevators and took the next free one to also go to the 3rd floor.

When the elevator reached the floor, Mike waited a second before peering around the corner to see if the hallway was empty. Sure enough, it was. So, Mike exited the elevator and strode calmly and quietly to the door of Rowland's suite. He looked around to make sure he was still not being observed, and placed his ear against the door. He heard two muffled voices speaking and, before he could be noticed by anyone, he hurried to the alcove two doors down, where anyone on that floor could get ice for the drinks they might consume from the mini-bar. The ice machine chugged along, dispensing its product over-and-over again, while Mike tried his best to hide in the darkness that surrounded the machine. He was able, however, to look down the hallway from the vantage point he had chosen. He kept his eyes on Rowland's door.

The time passed slowly. Mike was bored, so he took out his phone and brought up a game that he played while still keeping an eye on the door. Because his concentration on the game was split, he lost many times. Then, things started to happen. He looked at his watch; it was almost 1:30. He looked at the door, realizing that it was opening very slowly. Before long, Lund stuck his head out and looked up and down the hallway. When he was sure the hallway was empty, he stepped out quickly and motioned for Rowland to follow him. Shortly afterwards, Rowland stepped into the hallway, looking extremely disheveled. He was also obviously disoriented. Lund took his arm and directed him toward the elevator. When they were gone, Mike stepped down the hallway and stopped at Rowland's door. There was no sound now, but there was a sense of evil that Mike could not shake. He looked at the display above the elevator and saw that it had stopped at the 5th floor, the floor where Lund had his room.

Mike tried the doorknob of Rowland's suite. It was locked.

He took the stairs to the 5th floor and followed the hallway to Lund's room. The door was closed securely. He didn't try to open it, but he put his ear to the wood and listened intently. He heard the voices of Lund and Rowland speaking animatedly. He didn't know what to make of it. Instead of confronting Lund and Rowland, he took the stairs back to the 3rd floor and stopped outside Rowland's room again. Still no sound. Mike tried to open the door. It was still shut securely. He tried to force the door with his shoulder, but it was no good. The door was solidly shut. He took out a credit card that he hardly used and tried to jimmy the lock. It looked much easier on TV or the movies.

Suddenly, he heard the elevator start to move. He returned to the alcove and took up surveillance again. Very shortly, the elevator doors opened, and three unidentified men got out and moved swiftly to Rowland's door. The shorter one of the three took out a ring of keys, tried a number of them on the door, and finally unlocked it. The three unidentified men entered the suite quickly and closed the door silently behind them. Mike waited a moment, then crept down the hallway and stopped outside Rowland's door. He was afraid of being discovered, so he listened for a moment, heard nothing, then returned to the alcove.

He waited some more, but this time he didn't take out his phone to play games. Instead, he set up the video and waited patiently. Before he knew it, the door opened slowly and silently on its well-oiled hinges. Mike started the video recording on his phone; he was aware that something important was about to happen.

Soon, two of the men stepped out, the big burly ones, and one of them had something draped over his shoulder. It had shape to it, and substance, but it was wrapped in a sheet. The two burly men went swiftly past him. Mike withdrew into the darkness of the alcove and they did not discover his presence. It seemed as if they were headed for the service elevator in the back. After a moment, Mike heard the gears of the service elevator. He returned to his surveillance of the door.

Soon, the door opened again, and the short man stepped out quietly, looked around him, and when he was certain he wasn't being watched from his perspective, he peeled off the gloves he had been wearing and stuffed them in his coat pocket. He closed the door behind him and headed for the elevator at the front of the building. He took it down to the lobby. When Mike was sure they would not return, he went to Rowland's door again and listened some more. Total silence. He tried the door once more, but it wouldn't budge. Then he heard the regular elevator go into motion, and he returned to the alcove. Shortly, Lund and Rowland stepped out of the elevator and moved toward Rowland's room. Rowland had cleaned himself up and looked better than he had previously. They entered Rowland's suite, and Lund was in there for a very short minute. He took the elevator to the 5th floor. Mike waited a short minute, then crossed to the door of Rowland's suite once more.

He listened for any kind of sound, but there was nothing. He was tempted to knock and confront Rowland, but he was pretty certain that would get him nowhere. And besides, it might be dangerous. He had no doubt that Rowland was a dangerous man. When he was certain nothing further was going to happen, he went back to his room, opened his laptop, and wrote down what he had seen. He couldn't make head or tail of it, and tried very hard to put what he had seen together. The most problematic piece of the puzzle was the sheet-wrapped bundle slung over the shoulder of the big, burly guy, the only one it seemed who could carry the bundle easily, and not as a burden. Was Rowland that much of a dictator that his men would follow his orders without protesting? Of course, he paid them well, I'm sure of that, thought Mike.

But it was the bundle that truly concerned him. Was it a body? But of whom? Who could it be? Mike shivered with apprehension, for he was aware that the man he had decided to work for as a mole could possibly be a murderer. Crazy, he thought. This can't be true. Wait till he tells his editor. They'll have something to talk about later on in the day. He closed the laptop, stripped down to nothing, and climbed into bed. His mind kept churning along, so it took him quite a while to fall asleep.

3

Detective Brown and his partner were currently looking into the disappearance of a teenage girl by the name of Dolores Fisher, but they were getting nowhere so far. They had questioned the girl's parents, friends, and teachers, but there was no information that led them anywhere. When they returned to the squad room, Brown was trying to bring some order to the papers and files on his desk, when he came across the file on Litzy Baker, the poor prostitute who had jumped from a window. Or been thrown.

His young partner, McKenzie, saw him looking at the file, then wandered over in that direction. "Something?" he asked Brown.

Brown looked up and said, "What?"

"I see you're looking over that file there," McKenzie said, "and wondered if you've come up with something."

"Oh, this? Just ruminating."

"About what?"

"The fact that a young woman who had everything to live for would throw herself out of her bedroom window."

"You think she didn't do it?"

"I have my doubts."

"Then what do we do about it?"

"I don't know," Brown said. "Yet."

He sat back in his chair and thought some more, while McKenzie wandered back to his own desk. Although he was the new kid on the force, he had enough smarts to realize that his partner needed time to himself. McKenzie didn't know much about the Litzy Baker case, but he was willing to learn. After all, his job now was to follow in the footsteps of Brown and learn as much as he could without being a total nuisance.

On the other hand, Brown was finding it hard to articulate his thoughts, especially to his new partner. Brown was used to working alone; this partnership was something he was not familiar with. He leaned his elbows on his desk, and held his head in his hands.

After a moment, someone asked, "You all right?"

Brown lifted his head and said, "Yeah, sure, I'm fine. I'm just thinking."

"Looks to me like you had one helluva headache," the same detective said.

"Thanks," Brown admitted, "I'll remember that."

He looked over at McKenzie for a moment, then stood and walked over to him. "Hey, Mac, let's take a drive."

McKenzie grabbed his coat, and, without another word, left the squad room, with Brown, looking puzzled, right behind him. When they were in the car, Brown behind the steering wheel, McKenzie sat up in the passenger seat and asked, "Where're we going to?"

"Litzy Baker's apartment," Brown told him.

"Great," McKenzie said enthusiastically. "Let's get a move on."

Brown liked his enthusiasm. "Right you are," Brown agreed, and he turned the engine over, put the car in gear, and sped away, perhaps too fast for most traffic during the day.

***

The building looked the same: a brownstone located on the upper west side. But something felt different. Brown went on full alert. McKenzie, on the other hand, was unaware of anything unusual.

Brown had the keys to the building, so he led the way. They climbed the stairs carefully to the 3rd floor, and stopped in front of the door of Litzy Baker's apartment. The crime scene tape on the door was hanging limply; someone had entered without permission.

The door was open a couple of inches. Brown took out his gun; McKenzie followed suit. They burst into the apartment and caught a tall, lanky blond-haired young man bent over a suitcase on the floor of the living room. He looked up at their entrance and made a run for it, going through a bedroom window to the fire escape. Without a word, McKenzie went after him, and Brown disappeared out the front door, down the stairs, and through the front door of the building, around to the back. As he approached, he could hear the anonymous man and McKenzie clambering down the fire escape.

As the anonymous man's feet hit the concrete of the alley, he looked around and found Detective Brown with his gun out and aimed at him. There was only one exit from the alley, and Brown was standing in his way. He looked up and saw the big detective coming down after him. He had no place to run to anymore, so he stopped where he was and raised his hands in defeat. McKenzie hit the concrete and held his gun steady on the anonymous man from behind.

"That's a good boy," Brown said to the anonymous man. "Now, put your hands on your head and turn around."

The anonymous man complied. McKenzie snapped cuffs on him and took his arm and followed Brown back into the building and up into Litzy Baker's apartment. When they were safely inside, McKenzie pushed the perp on the couch, where the perp sat with a scowl on his face. Brown closed the door behind them and took a chair and sat in front of the perp.

"Okay," Brown started, "who are you?"

"I could ask the same of you guys."

Brown pulled out his badge and displayed it to the perp. "Now," he said, "does that answer your question?"

The perp shrugged.

"Now," Brown continued, "what's your name, so we can all be on the same page."

The perp didn't say anything.

"So," Brown said comfortably, "is that going to be the way it is?"

No answer from the perp.

"McKenzie," Brown said forcefully, "search him for any weapons and ID."

McKenzie went to work: he took the perp by the arm and pulled him up so that he was standing flat-footed; then McKenzie searched him: there were no weapons, but there was a wallet. He handed it to Brown, then pushed the perp back down on the couch until he was sitting on his hands.

"Hey," the perp protested, "watch how you handle the merchandise."

McKenzie smirked and pointed his thumb at the perp. "Funny guy," he said to Brown, with no actual mirth behind it.

Brown opened the wallet and took out the driver's license. "Jackson Blue," he read. "Impressive name."

The perp turned away. Brown leaned forward. "Why'd you run, Jackson?"

The perp looked Brown in the eyes. "I ran," he said, "because two guys with guns burst in on me. I didn't know who you were, and I was scared, so I ran. Wouldn't you do the same thing?"

"Not necessarily," Brown said.

"Let me have him," McKenzie said, with a mean growl to his voice. "I'll slap the attitude off him."

"We don't do things like that anymore," Brown said.

"Nobody has to know," McKenzie said. "I'll hit him where the bruises won't show."

"You guys sound like you're right out of Law and Order," Blue said, with a slight grin on his face.

"Watch your mouth," Brown said, "or I'll let Detective McKenzie have his way with you."

"Yeah, sure," Blue said, smirking mightily.

"Don't test me, Jackson," Brown warned. "Now. What were you doing here?"

Blue waited a moment, then said, "Collecting my things," grudgingly.

"Oh," Brown said, sitting back. "You're the guy whose clothes are here."

"That's right, O Mighty Detective," Blue said, with a sneer.

"Why is it nobody knows your name?" Brown asked.

"Because we wanted to keep it that way," Blue said. He was a wiry guy of indeterminate age: long shaggy blond hair, a thin face covered with some kind of growth that could be thought of as a beard. "You know what she did for a living," he continued. "I wanted to make sure nobody knew we were sleeping together."

"Her profession bothered you that much?" Brown asked.

"Sure," Blue responded. "Wouldn't it bother you?"

Brown didn't answer, he just stared at Blue without showing any signs of affectations about what Blue had said.

"Okay," Blue said. "I was picking up my things when you guys came storming in."

"You ever think about contacting the police?" Brown asked.

"Why should I?" Blue scoffed.

"Because maybe you have some information we could use to help find Litzy's killer," Brown said.

"I don't know anything," Blue objected. "I just want my things."

"This is a crime scene," Brown told him. "Didn't you see the tape on the door?"

"Sure," Blue said, "but why should I care about that?"

Brown shook his head. "You're an idiot," he told Blue. To McKenzie, he said, "Bring him in. We'll finish this interview down at the station."

"What's the charge?" Blue protested.

"Tampering with a crime scene," Brown said, and he stood up abruptly and headed for the door to the apartment.

McKenzie took Blue by the arm, hauled him to his feet, and dragged him out of the apartment in Brown's wake.

The door closed loudly behind them, shutting in the ghost of Litzy Baker.

***

When they got to the station house, McKenzie stopped at his desk to fill out the paperwork, while Brown took Blue's arm and escorted him to an interview room, where he placed Blue in a chair, unlocked one half of the cuffs, and secured it to a ring bolted into the table.

"You don't have to do that," Blue protested. "I'm not gonna do anything."

"This'll just make sure you won't," Brown assured him. Then he sat down in the chair on the other side of the table and asked, "Can I get you anything, Jackson? Coffee, tea, soda, water?"

"Nah," Blue said. "I'm okay."

"Good. Then let's talk."

"What about?"

"How long did you know Litzy?"

"What's that got to do with anything?"

"I don't know," Brown said. "Maybe everything. Maybe nothing. You didn't kill her, did you?"

"What? I thought she committed suicide!"

"Why would she do that?"

"I don't know. But I didn't touch her."

"Did you ever touch her? Besides sex, that is."

"What's that supposed to mean?"

"You look like a guy who's handy with his fists."

"I don't hit women," Blue said.

"Are you sure about that? My partner is running your name right now."

"Okay, okay. Maybe I slapped her a couple of times, but nothing serious."

"You really think that way?" Brown asked. "Because if you do, you're way past any kind of rehabilitation."

"What do you mean? I'm all right now. Then, I was on drugs and always angry. I didn't mean to hurt Litzy, but sometimes she wouldn't shut up, and I had to do something about it. Any guy'd be that way."

Brown shook his head slowly from side to side. "I don't think so, Jackson. You're a true, dyed-in-the-wool domestic abuser."

"Don't say that. I've cleaned up my act."

"Then tell me how long you knew Litzy."

There was a silence as Blue thought about it.

"It's not that hard a question, Jackson," Brown said. "How long did you and Litzy know each other?"

The door opened suddenly and McKenzie stepped through. Blue seemed relieved at first until he saw the papers in McKenzie's hands. McKenzie handed them to Brown, who perused them slowly. Blue began to sweat.

"What do we have here?" Brown said, with much interest. "A couple of DUIs, three domestic abuses, and one petty theft. Anything you want to say about your rap sheet?"

Blue remained silent.

Brown sat up in his chair and put the papers on the desk; he pushed them toward. Blue. "Looks as if you used Litzy as a baseball. Any comments on that?"

"Look," Blue said nervously, "it's not what you think..."

"It never is," Brown said as he laced his fingers behind his head. Without looking at him, he asked McKenzie, "What do you think, Mac?"

McKenzie smiled. "I think we got a bad 'un here."

"A bad 'un, eh?" Brown said. He leaned forward. "What was your relationship with Litzy?"

Blue shifted in his chair. "We met every once in a while and fucked."

"That's all?"

"That's it."

"Then why were you picking up your clothes?"

"Litzy was gone. I needed my stuff back."

"Why were they there in the first place?"

"What do you mean?" Blue asked, not able to meet Brown's eyes.

"A casual relationship does not usually allow for personal items in one's or the other's place."

"I had my own apartment, and she had hers."

"What? Did she keep tampons at your place?"

Blue crossed his arms and said, "I want a lawyer."

"You sure about that?"

"I haven't done anything, but you seem to think I have."

"It's just a thought," Brown said.

"Well, you can take that thought and shove it up your ass."

"Now, that's not a nice thing to say. Why don't any of her neighbors know a thing about you?"

"Should they?"

"It usually happens that way."

"We kept it secret," Blue said, "because we didn't want anyone else to know."

"Because you were embarrassed by her profession."

"I want a lawyer."

Brown picked up Blue's rap sheet and stood. "Mac," he said, "get this scum a lawyer." He turned and walked out of the room.

McKenzie leaned over the desk and put his face just a couple of inches from Blue's. "You just got on the wrong side of a very mean customer." He smiled again and then left the room.

Blue started sweating some more.

***

When they were in the corridor outside the interview room,

196

McKenzie asked, "You think you can get something out of this guy?"

"I hope so," Brown said. "We need every break we can get."

McKenzie appreciated the "we" Brown had used.

As they walked toward their desks, another detective stopped Brown and said, "The captain's looking for you."

Brown rolled his eyes and made a face, which caused the detective to giggle, which was his most endearing trait. At least, to women. Brown headed for the captain's office. He found the door open and gave it a couple of light taps.

The captain looked up from a file he was engrossed in. "Oh, Brown," he said. "Good. Come in and close the door behind you."

Brown did as he was told and moved further into the room.

He seemed to stand at attention when he was in front of the captain. The captain looked up and said, "Take a seat."

"Yes, sir," Brown said. He took one of the chairs that faced the captain.

The captain leaned back in his chair and said, "I understand you're still looking into the Litzy Baker case.

"That's right."

"Why? I thought it was ruled a suicide."

"I'm sorry, Captain," Brown said, "but there's something hinky about it that I can't put my finger on."

"What's hinky about it?"

"I don't know, Captain, that's the thing. I have this feeling about it that won't let me go. Call it intuition, if you want."

"But I can't justify using one of my cops on something that is so obviously a suicide."

"Listen, Captain," Brown said as he leaned forward in his chair, "give me a couple more days. If I can't find anything, then I'll close it."

The captain pondered for a moment, then said, "Okay," grudgingly. Forty-eight hours, but that's it."

Brown smiled and said, "Thanks, Captain. You'll be the first to know if I find anything suspicious."

"I better be," the captain said. "Now, get outta here."

Brown moved toward the door, but before he could open it, the captain asked, "How's McKenzie doing?"

Brown smiled again. "I think he'll do just fine."

"Good," the captain snapped. "Now get back to work."

Brown went out the door and over to his desk.

McKenzie met him there. "Everything okay?" he asked.

"Sure," Brown said. "He just wanted to know how you're doing."

"Oh, really? What'd you say?"

"I told him you were doing great."

McKenzie smiled. "You did? Thank you."

"Don't thank me. Just keep up the good work."

McKenzie smiled all the way back to his desk.

4

R owland arrived at LaGuardia airport at 2:15 pm and immediately took a car to his Manhattan building, where he took the elevator up to his office and did not say hello to his wife first. He asked for some coffee, and shortly afterward, his secretary, Miss Stanhope, served it to him as he leered at her and then disappeared through the office door.

Rowland sipped at his coffee while going over the events of last night. It was one of his greatest rallies. He told the crowd that there were many people who didn't like him and would try to stop him from becoming president. But he promised everybody in the crowd that if they attacked these rabble-rousers, he would pay for that persons court costs. Sure enough, one of the protesters was in the crowd, and when he opened his mouth, Rowland ordered security to escort him out. As he was being led up the aisle, a short, grizzled old man stepped out of one of the rows and punched the protester in the face. No charges were brought against the old man because he was under the wings of a demagogue who looked more and more as if he was planning to take over the country as a dictator.

And then his mind turned to darker matters: the whore he killed. How could he be so stupid? At least nobody saw it. He was very careful. He contacted his most loyal subsidiaries who carried out the cover-up in a moment's notice and without a word of complaint or questioning. The cunt would never be seen or heard from again. Of that, he was sure. After all, she laughed at his dick before it grew hard. And besides, by her laughing at it, his dick remained shriveled in an unnatural size for a man such as he. He was unable to forgive her, so he beat her and beat her, and then he grabbed a knife from the table delivered by room service. Her blackened eyes widened as he plunged the knife into her heart.

Blood came out of her mouth and dribbled down her cheeks as the life went out of her eyes. He sat by her dead body for close to an hour before calling his loyal associates. After all, he couldn't afford to lose his bid for the presidency because of a dead whore. Two dead whores, actually. He needed all his wits about him before he could do anything else. A dead whore was nothing but an inconvenience.

Of course, he would have to start slowly: get elected first, then give the people what they want for four years, then get reelected and take everything you gave them away. What a plan, he thought. I'm a genius, but first, I have to get elected. He finished his coffee, and suddenly, the door to his office swung open, and in came Albert Hanson. Rowland hadn't seen or spoken to him for at least two weeks, and Hanson was obviously so full of news that he hardly could contain himself, he was so ready to burst. Rowland had seen him like this so many times before, and since Hanson was his unofficial campaign manager, Rowland thought it best to humor him. He sat back in his ergonomic desk chair and smiled up at him and said, "Well, Al, what a surprise. What brings you here?" exuberantly.

"Don't give me that shit, Eddie," Hanson said, "you've been avoiding me for the past month..."

"Has it been that long?" Rowland asked wonderingly.

"Cut the crap," Hanson said, "we've got things to talk about."

"I know," Rowland said, "I've just been gloating to myself for a while."

"What about?"

"My successful campaigning."

"Okay. Yes, you've done well. But there's one thing you've forgotten about."

"Such as?"

Hanson paused for effect. Then he said, "Remember the debates? They're coming up very soon, and since you've been gone, a long string of republicans has appeared to give you some competition. Or haven't you noticed?"

Rowland swiveled his chair away from him. "Yes, I've noticed," he said grumpily. "What about them?"

"Well, don't you think you'd better start boning up on who they are? It's going to be tough to get around them---"

"I know," Rowland interrupted, "but I've got a game plan."

"Do you mind sharing it with me?"

"Sure, but not here."

"Where then?" Hanson demanded.

Rowland leaned forward and whispered, "Let's go to lunch."

Hanson asked, "Why are you whispering?" as the office door flew open and his family began to stream in.

He realized that Rowland had heard them coming before he did, for Rowland was quite able to split his focus in as many ways as he wanted, while Hanson remained focused on the subject under discussion at all times. He straightened up and moved away from Rowland before he could be engulfed in their welcoming routine.

Priscilla, the oldest, was first, followed by Daniel, the youngest, and then Roger, who was the classic middle child, forgotten and sometimes misplaced. Hanson stood by the window, with his back to the view, and observed the family dynamics:

Priscilla kissed her father chastely, making no body contact (Hanson wondered what had gone on between them), while the boys shook hands with him and belly-bumped, which was some sort of ritual between them, some macho thing that Hanson could never understand. Carlotta, the wife, was not there; Hanson knew she hated Rowland like rat poison. Why she married him, he would never know. She could have had anybody she wanted. But she chose Rowland: an enigma wrapped in a conundrum.

***

Carlotta Rowland, the wife of Eddie Rowland, sat alone in her isolated bedroom, which she preferred to the chaos surrounding her bastard of a husband. She was watching the news, first MSNBC, then CNN, and finally, her husband's favorite because it praised him so highly, Fox News. She was captivated by the buffoonery of her husband, his insignificance when it came to helping the people, who were totally enamored by his vulgarity and the fact that he didn't act like a politician. Instead, he pretended to act like the people who worshipped him, because he expected to become president by doing so. The republicans followed him because of the conservative values and conservative agenda he professed.

They didn't like him, but they followed him because they wanted the White House back after eight years of Charles Grant, the black man who had tried to take over the world. At least, that's the way Eddie explained it. His followers worshipped him as a god, while the Democrats wanted to crucify him.

Carlotta turned off the TV and started to pace angrily. If only she could understand what Eddie was trying to do. Maybe then, she could stand by him and support him. But his vulgarity and personal outlook disgusted her. She came from a poor family in Romania; she had worked her way up into modeling because of her startling looks. However, she couldn't seem to break into the American scene, which disappointed her greatly. Until she met Edward "Eddie" Rowland, a rich American who wanted to fuck her. She could tell right away by the bulge in his pants, but she kept him waiting until he asked her to marry him. Then she waited until after the wedding, and even then cock-teased him until he couldn't hold it in any longer and squirted all over her face. She laughed, and he laughed with her, then when he was hard again, he entered her for the first and last time. Having his fat body on top of her made her want to puke, but he was her ticket to America.

Shortly after she began her pacing, Maria Fernandez, her mother's best friend, a sturdily built woman of middle-age, came striding into the room. Maria had been with Carlotta since she was very small, and her advice was instrumental in leading Carlotta onto the straight and narrow.

"What is bothering you, child?" she asked in Spanish.

"Oh," Carlotta said in frustration, "it's that fat pig and his attempt to become president. Have you heard anything more ridiculous?"

"Yes, many times," Maria answered softly. "I have seen things in this world that would amaze even the most intelligent of us. Your husband is only exercising his God-given right. And what about you?"

Carlotta stopped in mid-stride. "What about me?" she asked, now even more confused.

"Are you going to remain here in isolation for his entire campaign? Or are you going to stand by his side and support him as a good wife should do?"

"Why should I support him? This is not what I signed up for."

"You will see how valuable this is. If he becomes president, you become First Lady. Which can become the second most powerful position in the United States. If you play your cards right."

Carlotta had to think that one over. After a moment, she asked, "You really think so?"

"Oh, most assuredly," Maria went on to assure her. "And I guarantee it, if you listen to me and not that fat idiot who calls himself your husband."

Carlotta stared at her with cold eyes. "You hate him as much as I do, don't you?"

"Much, much more. I've been waiting for this moment. Who do you think it was who put the notion in his head?"

Carlotta giggled. "You're kidding," she said.

"I am deadly serious," Maria said. "Once we are in the White House, keep feeding him those Quarter Pounders from McDonald's he loves so much, and sit and wait for his heart to burst."

"But the Vice President would then take over."

"We'll see about that. Just take my advice, and we will make you the most important woman in the world."

"You really think so?"

"My darling, I know so."

Carlotta nodded happily. "I'll do it," she said.

"That's my girl," Maria said, and took her in her arms.

***

The family reunion was not a typical reunion: the children clustered around Rowland, looking for some kind of approval from him. After all, he was still their father, even if—for some reason— he was not happy with them, except of course for Priscilla, who was still the apple of his eye; she stood to the side, watching indifferently the mild commotion which included her brothers, who wanted their fair share of their father's attention.

Hanson remained by the window, watching the parade of insincerity as it wafted through the room. Actually, he was faintly disgusted by the fawning over Rowland that showed how his children were not at all the happy, adjusted children they should be, what with Rowland's millions that were not as much as Rowland claimed.

Suddenly, the door to the office opened and Carlotta Rowland drifted into the room, a smile that was so fake her face looked as if it might crack open. She drifted over to the crowd surrounding Rowland, gently forced her way through, and crept up behind her husband and slithered her arms around him, delivering a kiss on his right cheek, which took him by surprise.

She whispered something into his ear, which made him faintly smile.

The children realized, in the presence of their stepmother, that they were outnumbered and outgunned, even by an individual presence such as Carlotta's. They backed off and stood around for a while, looking extremely uncomfortable, then they left the office without saying anything else. They knew that when Carlotta was around and acting this way, they were as invisible as the air they breathed. Hanson was of the same opinion. After another moment, while Carlotta indecipherably draped herself over her husband, Hanson sidled up to the door and went out silently. He would meet Rowland for lunch.

5

Mike Espinoza lay in bed, staring up at the ceiling, enjoying his solitude while his lover, Jake Gottlieb, showered. They hadn't seen each other in weeks because Mike had been on the campaign trail with Rowland, and when they reconnected, they fell into bed like two horny animals, fucking each other with asperity, feeling their juices shoot out of them with a great rush of joy and everlasting warmth. Just before Jake went into the shower, he gave Mike a phenomenal blowjob, which he was very good at, and when Mike came, he emptied his balls into Jake's mouth, and Jake swallowed him with contentment. In fact, he let out a slow "Ahhhhh" when he was finished.

Afterwards, Mike thought back to the moment in the hotel corridor when he suspected the men from Rowland's room were carrying a dead body. He hadn't known what to do. Should he have called the police, or just let it go? He surely couldn't do that. After all, if it was what he thought, then it was murder. Would it be too difficult to tell the New York police about it? He didn't see why not. Let them figure it out. That was their job, wasn't it?

Who was that detective he spoke to after Pedro's death? He couldn't remember the name, but he was sure the detective had given him his card.

So, he got out of bed and padded over naked to his desk in the corner. He was rummaging through the drawers, bent over, when Jake came quietly out of the bathroom. He saw Mike and instantly grew hard. He didn't think he should allow an opportunity like this to go by, so he crept quietly up behind Mike and grabbed him by the hips and inserted his hard dick into Mike's asshole. Mike was surprised at first, but when they got really started, he began to follow Jake's motions until they both came at the same time, and they were both loud lovemakers, so when they came together, they screamed together. Jake grabbed Mike's cock from behind and, while his cock was still up Mike's ass, pulled on Mike's cock until he squirted his semen all over the desk blotter. Now, they were both pleasurably spent and fell back on the bed together.

"I love you," Mike said to Jake.

Jake responded, "I love you, too."

And they lay in each other's arms for a while.

Finally, Jake asked, "What were you looking for when I came out of the bathroom?"

"Oh, that," Mike said, visibly upset. He sat up and looked over his shoulder at Jake. "When we were in Cleveland, I saw something I'm not very sure about."

Jake sat suddenly, put an arm around Mike's naked shoulders, and said, "What? Some juicy gossip? Tell me," excitedly.

"It's not exactly that..."

"What then?"

Jake was getting more and more excited.

So, Mike told him everything, every little detail. As he spoke, Jake's mouth opened wider and wider until—as the saying goes—his jaw hit the floor.

"Do you think what I'm thinking?" Jake asked.

"What are you thinking?"

"Do you think it was a body they were carrying out?"

"What kind of body?"

"A dead body, you idiot," Jake said mischievously, and he nudged

Mike with his elbow.

Mike couldn't help but laugh a little. "I don't know," he said despondently, "but I think so."

Jake became even more excited; he got up on his knees and flung his arms around Mike from behind. "A real live mystery," he practically squealed. "Do you know how wonderful that is?"

"Well," Mike said begrudgingly, "I don't know how wonderful it is…"

Jake started nibbling on his ear. "What are you going to do about it?"

"Nothing," Mike said, "as long as you're doing that."

"Oh, sorry," Jake said, and moved away from Mike, giving him some room.

Mike crossed his legs as unobtrusively as possible, since his cock had become erect from Jake's nibbling. Jake smiled politely, not having missed the state of Mike's cock; he would like to suck it dry and please Mike the way he had tried from the beginning of their relationship. But he knew not to distract Mike when he was concerned about something. Sex can wait a minute while more important matters are discussed.

"So, what're you going to do about it?" Jake asked.

"I don't know. I have to find the card of that detective I spoke to a little while ago."

"Do you think that's gonna help?"

"It couldn't hurt," Mike said. "I've gotta get ready," and he stood with his cock standing at attention.

Jake said, "Just a minute," and pulled Mike to him, taking Mike's cock in his mouth and sucking vigorously, until Mike came in his mouth and was relieved of all his tension. He fell back on the bed, his eyes closed from pleasure, and Jake covered him with a blanket.

"You don't have to go into the paper until later," Jake said. "Why don't you get some sleep?" He proceeded to give Mike a passionate kiss on the lips, which almost instantly put Mike to sleep. His gentle snoring filled the bedroom.

He looked down at Mike's sleeping figure for some time, then got dressed and left the apartment hurriedly. When out on the street, he made a phone call, a very secretive phone call, then took the train to 57th and Broadway, and followed 57th Street to Fifth Avenue, where he met someone who was just coming out of the Rowland Building. They went to a coffee shop not far away, and Jake told him everything Mike had seen while in Salt Lake City, and the man said he'd take care of it. Not to worry.

Then, they parted, and Jake walked slowly back to the train station, weeping copious tears, so much so that pedestrians passing him looked concerned, thinking he had just lost a very dear one.

They did not know, however, that his loss had not happened—just yet.

6

Julie Borstrand stood looking out of her bedroom window. She had already bathed and dressed and applied her make-up, but she was reluctant to leave and join the unwashed masses who swarmed the streets of New York City. She was nervous about tonight; it was the first of the many debates the Republican Party and its many contenders would hold to find a nominee for president.

She'd never realized how many contenders there would be; at least 17, with Bud Congreve leading the pack. He was the favorite, but soon she was hoping his dreams would fade quickly. He had once been governor of Florida, and his brother, Edgar, had been governor of Texas, then a very poor president for two uneventful terms, while their father had been a one-term president because of his complacency toward his constituents. She was sure Bud hoped to change the power of his family in his favor. She was sure Eddie would change everything in her favor.

And yet, she was still worried about him, for he was extremely unpredictable and unscrupulous. He'd shown that in many of his business dealings. He was a loose cannon, liable to do everything for himself, and nothing for anybody else. But even if he was nominated for president, which seemed a distinct—if very minor—possibility, she would pummel him in the election. She knew he could not beat her hands down, but he would try to make a good run for the presidency. It was up to her to make sure he remained on the sidelines; she was sure she could do that. After all, she was a politician, while Rowland was nothing but a thug, and would remain so in the White House if given half a chance.

Frankly, Julie thought, he was a menace and literally scared the hell out of her. She had put up with him when he supported her for office, but lately, he seemed to be getting further and further away from the plan they had agreed on so many months before. It seemed as if he was grooming himself for the presidency. That couldn't happen, she thought. She needed to make sure of that. There was a soft knocking on the door. Julie didn't turn in that direction but said, "Come in," softly.

The door opened, and her husband stepped in, almost timidly. His wife and he slept in separate bedrooms, mainly because Julie had discovered Robert's many philandering's a long time ago. Very early in their marriage, in fact. But Julie clung to him because she loved him for some reason, and she believed in him. She knew he would be president someday, and if he became president, then she would run for president herself someday.

"Good morning," Borstrand said. He took a step forward. "How did you sleep?"

"Not very well," Julie said. "Why do you ask?"

"Because I thought you might be nervous about tonight's debates," Borstrand explained, and he took another step forward.

Julie turned toward him. "Robert," she said, "why are you here?" and she crossed her arms in defiance. She didn't know why she became defensive in Robert's presence, but she was not going to let him manipulate her any longer. After all, she was running for president, wasn't she?

"I just thought I'd come and sit with you for a while," Borstrand said, "and we'd watch the debates together." He took another step forward.

"That won't be necessary," she replied. "I'll be watching it here in my bedroom."

Borstrand smiled disarmingly; he had a habit of that, Julie realized. "Couldn't I join you?" he asked, and he took another step forward.

"What do you want, Robert?"

"I ... I ... just ... want to be with you," Borstrand stammered. He took another step forward; he was now only a short distance from her.

"Why all of a sudden?" Julie asked aggressively. "Are your whores not available right now?"

"Don't be that way," Borstrand said admonishingly, taking another step forward.

"What do you expect? After all these years."

"I expect some kind of consideration, after all."

"You don't deserve it," Julie said, and turned to look out of the window again.

With her back to him, he was able to sidle up behind her quietly. She could feel him breathing down her neck. It still excited her. She was suddenly ashamed of herself, still feeling this way after everything he had done to her. He put a hand on her shoulder. She shrugged it off.

"Get out," she said.

"But Julie..."

"Go away."

"But you're my wife..."

"When has that meant anything to you? Now get out, or I'll call Bruce." Bruce was her bodyguard, a monster of a man, strong enough to break someone's neck with a slight twitch of his fingers.

It angered Borstrand to hear her threaten him with Bruce. He grabbed her shoulders and turned her around. Before she could do anything about it, he had her in his arms and was kissing her on the mouth, his tongue invading it, looking for her tongue. She was tempted to bite his off, but thought better of it. As his hand invaded her pants, she tried to fight him, but he was too strong for her. He pulled her toward the bed and threw her on it, then climbed on top of her. She struggled and struggled, but he was pinning her down. He suddenly pulled down her pants and panties and invaded her body with his cock. He was always good at lovemaking, so she was immediately turned on and embraced him, with her legs wrapped around his waist as he thrust his cock inside of her and slowly but surely fucked her to an oblivion she hadn't felt for a very long time. When he came, she came with him, bringing them as close together as they had ever been. Tears slipped down her cheeks as she grasped him to her, her arms holding him too close because she could feel his sudden change as he slipped outside of her and out of her grasp.

He climbed off the bed and almost stood there shamefacedly, with his pants down around his ankles, and his once rigid cock now limp and flaccid. He wasn't embarrassed the way she was, covering herself with a sheet from the now rumpled bed, and he pulled his pants up around his waist, stuffing his shirt inside, then tightening his belt. He looked down at her, her face averted from his, tears still streaming down her cheeks. He almost told he was sorry, but decided against it, for he was a proud man, and to admit he had raped his wife just now would be totally against his principles. So, he bent to touch her, but she pulled away from him, wrapping the sheet more closely around her. He stood straight again and made sure he was dressed properly, then quickly strode to the bedroom door and disappeared through it.

Julie sat there for some time, composing herself as best she could, wiping the tears from her eyes with the sheet around her until they stopped altogether. Then, she rose from the bed in a sort of daze, and wandered into the bathroom, where she removed what remained of her clothing, and stepped into the shower for the second time that day, and thoroughly scrubbed the stink of her so-called husband from her abused vagina. The water was as hot as she could take it, and she made sure every inch of her was scrubbed until there was practically no skin left on her otherwise misused body, a body that hadn't felt such pleasure in a long time because she believed in the sanctity of marriage and had never cheated on Robert. Her body tingled when she touched herself, and she instantly felt ashamed, for whatever anyone might say, Borstrand had raped her as surely as some punk on the street would rape an unsuspecting young woman. But she wouldn't tell anyone about it, and she certainly wouldn't press charges, for she was a smart politician and knew that it would only hurt her chances for the presidency. So, she would keep her mouth shut, and look like a good wife until she would take her first step into the White House as the first female president of the United States. Just the thought of it made her smile, and she knew she had to do what it took to get where she wanted to be. When she stepped out of the shower, she felt somewhat refreshed, but she still felt like the Whore of Borstrand, which was even worse than the Whore of Babylon. She literally wanted to strangle him; at that moment, she hated him more than she ever had before. He thought he could use her anyway he wanted to because he was of the male species, but he was undoubtedly a sad specimen. She still loved him, she knew when he fucked her like that, but when he was away from her, she felt as if she'd been destroyed by his wandering ways and his treatment of her, which was so despicable, she couldn't even speak. She was ashamed of herself; she hated herself almost as much as she hated him.

She took a towel from the rack and wiped herself down, taking special care of the tender spot between her legs. Robert Borstrand, ex-president of the United States, ex-governor of Arkansas, ex-mayor of Little Rock, was a rapist, but none of his followers would ever know. She would keep that secret to the grave. Not even their daughter would know, unless her father sexually abused her, which was unthinkable; he loved her deeply, and she loved and respected him. But if she ever found out about what had happened, she would literally die inside, so, she must not know. Ever.

7

The crime scene was pristine. Except for the dead body on the bed. And the blood all around it. A masterful job of murder. Or so the cops thought. But the one cop that mattered had not yet arrived. The bedroom was swarming with crime scene techs, photographs were taken from many different angles. The body lay there, his eyes closed forever, his face almost smiling with relief.

Finally, Brown, from homicide, trudged to the top of the stairs where the apartment was located, his faithful partner, McKenzie, right behind him. They entered the open door of the apartment, where police were gathered, not necessarily discussing the crime scene. Instead, they were mostly talking about their recent conquests at the cop bar around the corner. But they stopped talking when they saw the stern look on Brown's face and dispersed enough to allow him entrance. Brown didn't look directly at any of them, he simply stopped in the living room to observe the scene of a distraught young man on the couch, crying inconsolably, sobbing more like it, his body visibly shaking with distress.

Brown saw that the bedroom was crowded, so, he believed that the crime scene must be in there. So, he stepped into the bedroom, with McKenzie bringing up the rear. It was very obvious what had happened here, for, after all, a dead body, with what looked like two bullet holes in the chest, was lying there quietly, a splash of bright red surrounding his body and soaking the white sheets beneath him. There was no other disturbance that Brown could see; the body had been murdered while sleeping. A very nice way to go. He didn't see it coming. How peaceful it must have been after the two bullets ripped through the corpse's chest and into his heart. No screams, no cries for help, just simple death, uncomplaining, almost unrelieved bliss.

"Who found him?" Brown asked the crime scene tech.

"Guy in the living room. Name of..." He quickly checked his notes.

"...Jake Gottlieb."

"What's the relationship?"

"Boyfriends," the techie answered.

"Anything unusual about the scene?"

"Not really. Simple in-and-out, leaving a couple of bullets behind, of course."

"Any fingerprints?"

"A bunch, but I'm pretty sure they all belong to the corpse and the boyfriend."

"Eliminate them," Brown told him, as if he was producing some new magnificent idea.

"I was planning on doing just that," the techie said, and went back to work.

Brown looked at McKenzie. McKenzie said, "The boyfriend."

Brown nodded silently and led the way back into the living room.

A cop was standing by the boyfriend, questioning him and taking notes. Finally, he looked up from his note-taking and noticed Brown and McKenzie standing there, waiting for a chance to break into the conversation. The cop took a couple of steps backwards, allowing Brown to step in and open a new conversation.

"I'm Detective Brown," he told the boyfriend, and then gestured toward his partner, "and this is Detective McKenzie. We're sorry for your loss."

The boyfriend sobbed even louder.

"Do you mind talking to us now," Brown asked, "or would it be better another time?"

The boyfriend shrugged half-heartedly and said, "Now's as good a time as any," and he buried his face in his handkerchief, continuing to sob with every word he spoke.

"May I have your name, sir?" Brown asked.

The boyfriend hiccupped an answer. "Jake … Gotlieb."

"Can you tell us what happened?"

"I don't know what happened. I came home around five o'clock and found him lying there … all … shot … up," and he burst into tears again.

"Did your boyfriend have any enemies?"

"Of course, he did. He was a journalist, and he angered a lot of lowlifes."

"Anyone in particular?"

"I couldn't say. He never shared his work with me," Gottlieb lied shamefacedly.

Brown pulled out a card and handed it to the boyfriend. "I know this is a very difficult time, Mr. Gottlieb, but if you can think of anything else that might be important, please give me a call."

The boyfriend looked at the card in confusion, trying to bring the words into focus. Brown and McKenzie walked away. The boyfriend looked after them, already knowing more than the detectives, but that didn't stop him from lowering his face into an already sopping wet handkerchief and sobbing some more.

***

Brown and McKenzie left the crime scene shortly afterwards, and as they were approaching their car, McKenzie asked, "What do you think?"

"I don't know," Brown said, "but something stinks to high heaven here."

"You think?" McKenzie asked.

"I know," Brown said. "The boyfriend knows more than he's saying."

"How can you tell?" McKenzie asked.

"Just a feeling," Brown said. "But I'm usually right." He opened the driver's side door and slipped behind the steering wheel. McKenzie slipped in next to him. Brown started the car. "I think we should visit the editor of his paper."

"Whatever you say, boss," McKenzie said.

They drove away from the crime scene.

***

The newspaper office was in confusion, journalists running back and forth from their computers to the managing editor, filing reports, sending them off via e-mail to important officials, trying very hard to compete with co-workers and win the day. There seemed to be no rhyme or reason in the way they worked, at least to Brown and McKenzie, who stood in the doorway, looking around in bafflement. When they were finally able to stop someone, flash their shields, and ask who they should talk to, they were directed to the office of Terry Wainwright, managing director of The Tribune, located at the rear of the upper landing.

The door to the office was closed, but they could see through the glass that Terry Wainwright was on the phone, screaming orders into it. Brown knocked politely, flashing his shield through the glass. Wainwright saw them and gestured for them to come in. The piercing timbre of Wainwright's voice made them hesitate before stepping over the threshold. Wainwright continued shrieking into the phone for another minute or so. Brown stood, embarrassed, while McKenzie smiled behind him. They didn't know what to do except stand there and listen to Wainwright's abuse as it flowed smoothly from his lips, under a quite impressive moustache.

Finally, Wainwright slammed down the phone and turned his craggy face to the two detectives. He exhaled and said, "Well, that felt good," then offered the detectives chairs across from his desk.

Brown took one of them; McKenzie remained standing. Wainwright sat behind his desk, opened an ornate humidor, and without asking permission, lit a cigar. The acrid fumes instantly filled the room, and Wainwright settled back in his ergonomic chair and let out a plume of smoke from his mouth that almost made Brown choke and made McKenzie suppress a cough. Once Wainwright settled, he turned to the detectives and asked, "So, what can I do for you gentlemen?" in his official pompous attitude.

"We're here about one of your reporters---" Brown started.

Wainwright interrupted with, "Mike Espinoza," letting smoke curl from his already smug mouth.

"You know?" McKenzie asked.

"We're a newspaper," Wainwright said, with a small smile. "We have reporters throughout the city, looking for stories..."

"I understand that," Brown said, "but did you know he was murdered?"

"Of course," Wainwright said, taking another puff of his cigar. "What do you think all this chaos is about?"

"We were wondering," McKenzie said.

"We're devoting an entire issue to Mike," Wainwright went on. "Great reporter. What a tragedy."

"You liked him?" Brown asked.

"Everybody liked him," Wainwright said. "He was not only a great reporter, he was a great kid."

"How long had he been working here?" Brown asked.

"About seven years," Wainwright said. "Maybe a little longer, but he made quite a name for himself."

"He must have," Brown said, "to warrant an entire issue."

"Well," Wainwright said smoothly, "this is the first time one of our major reporters was murdered in such an ostentatious way."

"You mean you've had other reporters' deaths?" McKenzie asked.

"Yes, quite a few," Wainwright said, "but they were in the usual way."

"What's the usual way?" McKenzie asked.

"Drive-by shootings," Wainwright explained. "Bodies dropped at our front door. Cars run over roads and over bridges. That kind of thing."

"I see," McKenzie said speculatively.

Brown asked, "But did Espinoza have any threats recently?"

"Not that I know of," Wainwright said.

"What was he working on?" Brown asked.

"Is that relevant?" Wainwright asked.

Brown lost his temper. "Of course, it's relevant," he said strongly. "This is a homicide investigation. What else did you think it could be?"

"Sure, sure," Wainwright said, "I obviously lost my head there for a second. Even though I may not look it, I still feel for the loss of Mike. Please excuse my insensitivity." He opened the bottom drawer of his desk and pulled out a large sheaf of paper. He tossed it on his desk and said, "This is what he was working on. It's all yours."

"Can we take it with us?" McKenzie asked hungrily.

"It's all yours," Wainwright said. "I have plenty of copies."

McKenzie picked up the papers and put them under his arm. He didn't say thank you.

"If there's nothing more, gentlemen," Wainwright said, "I have a great deal of work to do. So, if you'll excuse me…"

Brown stood up and handed Wainwright a card. "If you think of anything else, you'll let us know."

"Certainly," Wainwright said, and he took the card and put it in his top drawer.

Brown and McKenzie moved toward the office door.

Before they got there, however, Wainwright asked, "You will be discreet about those papers, won't you?"

Brown turned around and looked at him. "In what way?"

"They haven't been published yet. I need you to give me your word that you won't say anything about them to anyone."

"They're that good, huh?" McKenzie asked.

"They're dynamite, gentlemen," Wainwright assured them. "Please don't release them to anyone outside of this investigation. Understood?"

"Yes, sir," Brown said deferentially, and he and McKenzie disappeared out the door.

Wainwright watched them go, through the glass of his office, then turned to his phone, picked it up, and started barking orders again.

8

Julie Borstrand had remained in her bedroom all day, having her meals brought into her by her loyal assistant, Mary Riley, who wanted her to break the glass ceiling by becoming the first female president, a step forward in the fight for women's liberation. After all, she was a diehard feminist who staunchly believed that women were better than men in every way; that didn't make her a lesbian—she knew men had a purpose in life (to help repopulate the world)—plus, she loved the feel of a cock in her pussy, and that would never change. But, she simply believed that a woman's character—most women, that is—was better than a man's in every way, shape, and form.

That day, however, she knew that something untoward had happened between Julie and her prick of a husband, but she was too discreet to ask any questions. She simply knocked on the door and, when told to come in, she brought the tray in for her lunch, and then for her dinner, and when Julie buzzed for her, she returned to the bedroom and took the trays away. She could see in Julie's face that something very upsetting had happened, because Julie wore her heart on her sleeve, something that might keep her from the White House, even though she was the most experienced for the job at hand, and everyone seemed to know that, except for that dumb shit Eddie Rowland, who was intent on keeping women in the kitchen and the bedroom, just like the men in the past had wanted them. Times had changed, but Rowland hadn't changed with them.

When the debate came on at 9:00 that evening, Julie tuned in to MSNBC and watched eagerly. She hadn't spoken to Eddie in a long time, assured that he would do what they had agreed upon, and he certainly did his job by attacking all his competitors, especially Bud Congreve, her principal rival. He found smarmy names for all of them, calling them out in front of a huge audience that also included the television viewers. He was masterful with his remarks, even though they were sometimes vulgar, and, at other times, just plain bad taste. But he continued, with some of the live audience applauding his disgustingly bad taste, and then, turning against him and booing. And the booers outnumbered the applauders, which was a good thing, thought Julie, because she realized most of them would vote for her.

It continued for more than two hours, Rowland's vituperations against his competitors growing stronger by the minute. His mind was obviously on overdrive, although his stupidity remained foremost in Julie's mind. She had chosen the right man, she thought, for the job at hand. Rowland was among the world's great hypocrites, a true man of himself and no one else, who believed that he could overcome any adversity just by being himself and looking down on everybody else. He was showing his true colors that night, while a significant minority of followers cheered him on. He was becoming a dictator of the first order, while those who were against him laughed at him and proclaimed him a buffoon who resembled Mussolini in many ways. Yes, she had chosen the right man, but he was beginning to scare her.

Rowland was a juggernaut waiting to happen. Julie could see that he had now become a danger to herself and the world around him. She was tempted to call the whole thing off, but she knew it was too late. The beast had been released.

The tears that rolled down her cheeks unexpectedly surprised Julie. She wiped them away with her hands, but they just kept on coming; she couldn't understand why. Then it hit her like a thunderbolt: in normal days, she would have sat with her husband and discussed what was happening, but instead, she sat alone, wondering at the absurdity of what was happening. Her husband had raped her earlier that day, and because of that, she sat alone, watching an idiot like Eddie Rowland make his sudden bid for the presidency, destroying everyone around him with smart-alecky names he thought up, smashing each and every one of his competitors in the face with words that inflicted pain. She saw at that moment how cruel and evil a man could be. Yes, Eddie Rowland was the Beast come to life.

And he stood there, with that smug smile on his face, drinking in the admiration that emanated from his followers, believing now that he stood a chance of winning the White House.

She saw that look in his eyes, the look of a challenger who will not be overcome, the look of a man who seeks the world as his own and will not be put down. Although that's what Julie thought of him now: as a mad dog who needed to be put down. It was now her job to see that Rowland never got into the White House. The danger to the country was too overwhelming for her to laugh at Rowland; she needed to do something about it. The threat was much too real.

She watched as if she was watching a train wreck: fascinated by what was happening, too hypnotized to turn away. Rowland was doing his job, systematically at first, then with venom and torpor filling his mouth, then with cruel intensity, until his competitors seemed to be weakening in front of everyone.

They were trying to abide by the rules, but Rowland wouldn't let them: his words punched them in their faces, as if they were in a boxing match. Soon, if things kept up this way, they would have to call for a Technical Knockout. Rowland would be the last man standing. Julie couldn't let that happen.

***

Bobby Borstrand was in a miserable mood that day. It was not as if he was ashamed of himself for having sexually molested his wife, but he suddenly realized that whatever goodwill he had helped to preserve with her had forever been broken by his unreasonable lust. He thought of himself as a sexually proficient man, even for his age, but he was not able to control his urges. For some reason, he had desired his wife that morning—something that was unlike him and had been for a very long time—but it had gone all wrong when she had resisted him so strongly. She put up a good fight, he thought, but she was still not strong enough to overcome him when his mind was made up. He had wanted her desperately. He had wanted, for some unexplainable reason, to possess her as he had in the early days of their relationship. He had wanted them to be in love again, he had wanted her to want him as much as he wanted her, but it was no good. He had spoiled everything once again. He would not admit it to anyone, but he hated himself for being the goddamned fool he was.

He went through his daily routine as if sleepwalking, and when it was time for the debates, he stopped momentarily in front of Julie's bedroom door, then thought better of disturbing her, when in fact she probably wouldn't have answered in the first place. He spent the rest of the day locked up in his own bedroom, watching the debates from there just as his wife was doing from her bedroom, keeping score on a piece of paper as if it was a baseball game, making a stroke behind each name of the candidates who had scored points against Rowland. By the time they were over, Borstrand had put more strokes by Rowland's name than any of the other candidates, and he smiled when he thought back to the time Julie had come up with the scheme.

She told it to him in his office up in Harlem, very excited with what she thought was the genius of it, and while Borstrand had smiled at her patronizingly, just waiting for the moment he would burst her balloon. She became dumbfounded when Borstrand told her that he thought Eddie was a loose cannon who could never be trusted. They argued through the night, but Julie won the argument simply because she had more stamina than her husband and lasted throughout the night, while Borstrand nodded off in his desk chair quite frequently until he finally cried "Uncle!" and got up and crossed to his sofa against the wall and went into a very deep, deep slumber. Frankly, he didn't know what had happened to Julie because when he woke up shortly after 9:30 a.m., she was gone. He tried many times throughout the day to call her, but she never picked up.

As was his nightly routine when he was at home, he brushed his teeth thoroughly, having flossed them right after dinner, which—unfortunately—he had eaten alone, then got undressed, stood naked before the full-length mirror on the wall of the bathroom—something that Julie had insisted upon having so she could watch her diet carefully, and if she put on a few pounds, could deal with them before anyone else noticed—and looked at himself and the erection that had been lasting through the debates when he thought about the sex with Julie earlier in the day— something that he would never have thought possible a week earlier—and proceeded to masturbate to the thought of his wife's pussy.

He knew he was a sexual deviant, but—with all the therapists he had spoken to over the years—he also knew that there was no cure for it while he remained conscious. His testosterone had been backed up for some time now, and if he didn't relieve the pressure, he might do something to a stranger that he had already done to his wife. He got into his pajamas, crawled into bed, and turned out the light. He put his hands behind his head and stared up at the ceiling with a smug smile on his careworn face; he knew he was safe because Julie would not report it to the police. If she wanted to be president, that is. Borstrand had faith in her, because from the first moment she entered the White House, her ambition had taken over, and he could smell the longing for greatness emanating from her pores.

He turned over and went to sleep.

***

After the debates, when Rowland had finished shaking hands and being congratulated by members of the audience, he was met backstage by Al Hanson who shook his hand vigorously and said, "Great job, Eddie. But don't forget, you've got to keep putting on the heat. Don't let up, keep pushing and you'll become the republican nominee without any sweat," while they moved toward the limo waiting for them at the stage door entrance.

When they were in the limo and it had driven away, Hanson pulled out a sheet of paper from the inside pocket of his suit coat and started going over the pros and cons of Rowland's performance that night. While Hanson was doing this, Rowland stared at him in disbelief. He finally said, "But you told me I'd done a great job."

"That's true," Hanson said, "but there's always room for improvement," and he went on, going through his long list of dos and don'ts.

It was at that point that Rowland stopped listening and stared out the window at his city passing by. He thought of the night Carlotta had joined the campaign: when they were alone, she pulled his pants down and sucked him off. Frankly, it was the only time he could ever get hard. Whenever the woman who was working on him would put her lips to his cock, he would become erect enough to fuck them. Carlotta, however, did not like Rowland's cock inside her, so she blew him when she wanted something. He wasn't aware of this, so he remained oblivious while he came in her mouth and she sucked out every drop of his sperm from his balls, giving them a nice pat when she was done.

Even though she did this willingly, she did not get any pleasure from it; her pussy remained dry, and if he had tried to fuck her, he would have found it difficult to enter her. But he enjoyed it, even more than when he had fucked her at the beginning.

After a moment, he realized that Hanson was asking him a question, so he turned to him as he slowly came out of his pleasant memory, and said, "What was that, Al?" in a soft murmur that somehow exposed what he was thinking of to Hanson, although Hanson was not aware of the details and maybe someday Rowland would tell him, in order to make Hanson envious of what he had, which was a part of Rowland's DNA; he was always trying to outdo those around him, even when they were obviously above him in every way imaginable.

"You weren't listening to a word I said, were you?" Hanson asked irritably.

"Sure, I was listening!" Rowland insisted.

"Then what was the last thing I said?"

"Let's forget about that for now, Al, just tell me what you asked."

"Okay," Hanson said, with a shrug. He looked straight ahead, over the driver's shoulder, at the road ahead of them. "Where was Carlota tonight?"

Rowland smiled and said, "She wasn't feeling well. Her stomach was full of my spunk," and he laughed uncontrollably.

Hanson turned to his old friend and stared at him for a moment, then asked, "Is that what you're going to tell the press if they should ask?"

Rowland's laughter stopped, and he said, "Would that be a legitimate question?"

Hanson shrugged again. "I don't know," he told Rowland honestly, "but nowadays they can ask most anything."

"Well then," Rowland said, "I'll think about it when the time comes," and he turned away to look out the window again.

After a moment, Hanson said, "You understand we have a long road to go, Eddie. It's not going to be easy, but you have to eliminate as many of your competitors as possible."

"Not easy?" Rowland said, scoffing. "It's going to be a cinch. Those guys are so simple-minded, they don't know whether they're coming or going. I can wrap them around my little finger."

"It's not going to be that easy, Eddie," Hanson said. "You've got to stay focused for once."

Rowland finally looked at him. "You mean," he said, "you think I have trouble focusing?"

"That's right," Hanson said. "Even when you talk about yourself sometimes, you get distracted and leave the room without saying anything to the others who are there. It's not a very good political move. You have to stay laser-focused."

"You don't think I was laser-focused tonight?" Rowland asked.

"Not all the time," Hanson told him. "You're so full of yourself sometimes that you lose your attention to something else, and therefore, you lose the attention of the world. You've got to stay razor sharp."

"I know, I know," Rowland said impatiently. "You don't need to tell me that all the time."

"Then stay the course, man," Hanson insisted. "You could be president of the United States, the most crucial and important role in the world. In fact, you could change the world with one swipe of your hand. You don't seem to understand how important this is. We're all depending on you, Eddie. You can make the world your playpen if you try hard enough."

Rowland started to say something, but Hanson continued before he could get a word out.

"Think about it, Eddie. You can get to a point where you can control the governments of the world. You can be the most important man in the history of the United States. Don't you understand, man? Don't you see where your future lies? I'm behind you 100 per cent. But you have to do what I tell you to do. If you want to be president, you have no other choice. If you don't believe me, just look at the polls. You're wiping the floor with the rest of them. They're struggling just to stay in the race. You've got an iron fist that can give you the upper hand. As the saying goes, the world is your oyster."

There was silence in the car for a moment.

Then Rowland turned to his old friend with tears in his eyes and asked, "You really think it's possible?"

"I know it, my friend," Hanson assured him.

Rowland turned away for a second to surreptitiously wipe the tears from his eyes—something he very rarely had to do—then turned back and said, "You've got it. I'm in your hands."

Hanson smiled and gave him a playful punch in the arm.

They were just two boys playing with their erector set.

9

Brown and McKenzie sat at their separate desks and read Mike Espinoza's reports from the Rowland battleground, which he had been spying on for the past few weeks. They were quite revealing, and some of it was even hair-raising. They compared notes, especially about the possible homicide emanating from Rowland's hotel room in Ohio. Before they did anything else, Brown made a call to the Salt Lake City PD and spoke to a Detective Aronson; he asked if there were any missing prostitutes lately. Aronson didn't know what to answer right away—there was a long silence on the other end of the line—but finally he asked the question all detectives like to ask: "What's this about?" and Brown filled him in on as much as he could get away with.

After he was finished, Aronson hesitated for another couple of minutes, then said, "Well, as a matter of fact, Detective Brown, we've had a rash of prostitute killings in the last month. Plenty of young women tossed aside like so much garbage. Not that the public really cares about such people. We've been working on the cases when we could, but there's only so much manpower around here. I suppose your budget is a lot bigger than ours."

"Not by much, I'm sure," Brown said. "How many prostitutes are we talking about?"

"Five, to be exact," Aronson said.

"Any particular area of the city?" Brown asked.

"All in midtown," Aronson said, "which is usually the place they work out of."

"Any leads on the killer?" Brown asked.

"Not a one," Aronson said. "You got anything for me?"

"Not yet," Brown told him, "but I may have something in the future."

"Sure," Aronson said skeptically, "keep me in the loop."

They shot the shit for about two minutes or so, then they said goodbye, and Brown hung up. McKenzie was standing by Brown's desk and asked, "Well?" eagerly.

"Nothing right now," Brown said, "but let's keep on looking." He read some more, then called McKenzie back to his desk. "When was Rowland in Salt Lake City for his rally?"

"I'm not sure," McKenzie said. "A couple of weeks ago, I think."

"Do you know what hotel he was staying at?" Brown asked.

"Let me look," McKenzie said, and he rushed back to his desk, shuffled through some papers, then returned to Brown's desk in a hurry and said, "The Marriott."

"For a candidate for president, his digs are not very luxurious," Brown said. He mused for a little bit more, while McKenzie stood beside him, then picked up the phone and put in a call to the Salt Lake City Marriot; he introduced himself, then asked if Eddie Rowland had stayed there recently. The clerk was hesitant at first, then blurted out the truth: Rowland had been there a week- and-a-half ago.

Brown hung up and turned to McKenzie and said, "Could be the same time as the murder of the prostitutes," then picked up the phone and talked to Aronson again, who told him that the murders were around two weeks or so. When Brown hung up with a smile, he turned to McKenzie and said, "Ready for lunch?"

McKenzie said yes, and they hurriedly left the squad room.

They walked two blocks to a diner frequented by cops, and after they were seated in a booth and had ordered their food, Brown asked, "So? What do you think?"

"I'm probably thinking the same thing you're thinking," McKenzie told him, "but I'm not sure."

"Okay," Brown said, "that's fine. Then let me start." He took a sip of water, then went on, "It looks as if we've got a good case against Eddie Rowland."

"You think?"

"Don't you? He's a big-time manipulator and crook. Would he stop at murdering someone? I don't think so."

"But he's running for president…"

"What difference does that make?" Brown asked. "Some presidents have been the biggest crooks imaginable. Look at Nixon."

McKenzie shook his head and said, "You've got a point. What should we do about it then?"

"You scared of getting your hands dirty?" Brown asked.

McKenzie took offense. "What's that supposed to mean?"

"Now don't get your panties in a twist," Brown said, "all I want to know is if your able to go after a bigshot like Rowland. Because if you're not, I'll go it alone."

"Are you serious?"

"Yes," Brown said. "Are you?"

McKenzie thought about it as their food arrived, then, when they were alone, he said, "I'm in."

"Good."

McKenzie, after he swallowed a huge bite of burger, said, "How do we start?"

"Good question," Brown said. "Do you think we should tell the captain?"

"I'm not sure about that," McKenzie said. "He might not like it."

"On the other hand, he might," Brown said. "I know for a fact that he's a Democrat and hates Rowland like rat poison."

"But is that enough?" McKenzie asked.

"It might be," Brown said. "Let's think about it some more."

As they finished their lunches, they ruminated over the problem. The waitress asked what they would like for dessert. McKenzie asked for an apple pie. Brown asked for more coffee.

When the waitress was gone, Brown said, "You've got a big appetite."

"I'm a big guy," McKenzie said. "Haven't you noticed?"

The apple pie arrived, and McKenzie dug in as if he hadn't eaten in a couple of years. Brown was amazed at his stamina.

After a moment, he asked, "Well? What do you think?"

McKenzie's mouth was full of apple pie when he said, "It's your call," flakes from the pie spewing into the air.

Brown turned away as he sipped at his coffee and said, "I think we should talk to the captain."

"You got it," McKenzie said, another shower of flakes from the pie entering the atmosphere.

***

When they got back to the station, they went immediately to the captain's office. He was busy, so they waited patiently while the captain concluded his business. When the captain was ready for them, Brown strode in confidently, while McKenzie hesitated before crossing the threshold. The captain looked at them quizzically, and Brown told him about what they'd discovered from the writings of Mike Espinoza.

The captain listened intently, and when Brown was finished, he looked at both of them and asked, "So. You think you got something on Rowland?"

"Well, don't you?" Brown insisted.

"It sounds good," the captain said, "but you're gonna need to tread carefully."

"I'm aware of that," Brown said, his pride hurt. "I've been a cop for a long time now."

"Not as long as I have," the captain said. "But if you think you can do this as unobtrusively as possible, I'll give you a few weeks. Say three. That should be enough to get the goods on him."

Brown stood and said, "Thanks, Cap," and he strode—again confidently—to the door.

McKenzie stood there in the middle of the office, not sure what to do.

"Something wrong, McKenzie?" the captain asked.

"No, sir," McKenzie said. "Just wondering where my loyalties lie."

"What the hell does that mean?" the captain asked exasperatedly.

"Well, Cap," he began.

"McKenzie," Brown said warningly. "What do you think you're doing?"

McKenzie shook his head and said, "Nothing. Just wondering."

"Well," the captain said, "do your wondering outside of my office. That's what you're getting paid for. Now, shoo!"

"Yes, Cap," McKenzie said and followed Brown into the squad room.

Brown stopped him and asked, "What was that about?"

"Nothing," McKenzie muttered and walked timidly to his desk.

Brown watched him curiously, then went to his own desk and got to work.

***

As the weeks rolled by, and Edward Rowland made sure he was the last man standing among those reaching for the presidency, and Brown and McKenzie, as unobtrusively as possible, were trying to destroy the reputation of that man, word came down to Al Hanson that an investigation of his best friend and would-be president was being pursued by two of New York's Finest. Something had to be done about it. But he just wasn't sure what. He pondered the situation for a very long time, then decided to talk to Rowland about it. After all, this was his campaign, and he should be informed of what was going on around him, even if he was completely clueless about anything outside of his orbit.

Hanson tried to get in touch with Rowland all day, off and on, but Rowland didn't pick up his phone, and Hanson was sure he would get in touch with him soon. But he needed to get in touch with him right now, in order to talk to him about the possible trap they might find themselves in if the NYPD's investigation got too close. He looked up the two detectives, Brown and McKenzie, who were handling the case, and he found out that the young one, McKenzie, who had been a detective for only a couple of months, came from a family of construction workers who reliably voted republican every election. They wanted McKenzie to join a construction crew, but the young man was more interested in police work, so they backed off and let him do his own thing. It was possible that McKenzie would be able to be influenced by the Rowland campaign gang.

He tried Rowland again, and after three tries, Rowland finally picked up. The urgency in Hanson's voice was enough to convince the big man that they needed to meet because something was obviously brewing, and he became worried for a second. But since Rowland was Rowland, the worry left him two seconds after he hung up with

Hanson and watched a very young hooker suck his cock. She was doing a good job, he thought, but his dick was finding it difficult to get hard, and he finally threw her some money and told her to get lost. She got dressed and ran from the room, happy to be anywhere that wasn't with him, and then he started to think some more, which was always dangerous for him to do, and he finally stepped into a shower and tried very hard to rub his cock clean from the hooker's saliva, but he was having a hard time getting to his dick over his belly. He should have paid the whore more to wash his cock, but it was too late now. So, he took the shower head out of its holder and sprayed his cock until he was pretty sure the germs from the hooker were gone. Then, when he stepped in front of the mirror, he looked at himself critically and discovered that he was a reasonably attractive man for his age, something that no one else would even consider. But he was happy with the way he looked. He'd always been devilishly handsome. That's why he got all the women he wanted, but it never occurred to him that it was because of his money, not his looks.

When he was dressed, he grabbed a cab to his building and was surprised to find two cops waiting for him. One was black, the other red-haired and full of freckles. They flashed their badges and introduced themselves as Brown (perfect name for the black cop) and McKenzie, Irish to the core. Rowland asked if they could wait a few minutes, then rushed into his office, picked up the phone, and called Al Hanson, who didn't pick up. Where was he when you needed him? He grabbed himself some coffee and thought about his situation. It didn't seem good, in his mind, but he was going to have to bluff it out. He was good at that. He was a bullshitter from way back. He knew exactly what to do, and he would do it, no matter the consequences. After all, he was Eddie Rowland, the King of New York. Nothing could touch him. He called his secretary and told her to show the gentlemen in. They came ambling in, Brown cocksure of himself, McKenzie not so certain, and they sat down in the visitors' chairs, and Rowland asked if he could get them anything, and they said no, they were fine.

"So, detectives," Rowland said amiably, even though he was sweating like a pig and his dress shirt was already soaked, "what can I do for you?"

Brown noticed the sweat oozing from Rowland's pores almost immediately and enjoyed the pressure on Rowland that he and McKenzie instilled. He looked over at his partner, who seemed to be oblivious to the reaction they were getting from Rowland, and then turned back to Rowland and said, "Well, we have a few questions, Mr. Rowland," with a smile.

"What's the idea?" Rowland demanded. "Am I in trouble?"

"I don't know, Mr. Rowland," Brown said, his smile remaining. "Are you?"

McKenzie interrupted. "This is just a primary investigation, Mr. Rowland," he said, his tone light and unaffected. "Nothing to worry about."

"Well, that's nice to hear, gentlemen," Rowland said, "but usually the presence of two detectives in my office is uncomfortable for me."

"I can understand that, sir," McKenzie went on, "but there's really nothing to be worried about."

Rowland smiled painfully and said, "Well, ask your questions, gentlemen," shifting uncertainly in his ergonomic desk chair.

McKenzie looked over at Brown, the senior detective present, and then shifted his eyes away to look out at the view from Rowland's large window.

Rowland looked over at Brown, who was still smiling broadly, and said, "Well, gentlemen, what is it?"

"A situation has come to our attention," Brown began. "It might involve you, it might not."

"I'm at a loss, detective," Rowland said shakily. "What situation?"

Brown pulled out his pad, turned a few pages quickly, and then pretended to refer to his notes for Rowland's benefit. "It seems that while you were in Salt Lake City," he continued, "someone noticed suspicious activity coming from your hotel room."

Rowland chuckled nervously. "Suspicious activity?" he responded. "What are you referring to?"

"Well," Brown said, "I'm not really sure, but it seems as if some suspicious men met in your hotel room and carried something suspicious out. Do you know anything about that?"

Rowland shook his head and said, "Where do you get your information?"

"I'm afraid we can't tell you that," Brown said.

"Well," Rowland said, "this sounds like something the Salt Lake City police should be interested in..."

"They are," Brown assured him comfortably, "and so, since you're here in New York, they decided to contact us to do some investigation from this end."

Rowland sat forward and said, "I must say, gentlemen, you're making me very nervous. Whoever is spreading such vicious rumors about me should be reported. After all, an election year is coming up, and my competition will say anything to ruin my chances."

"So, there's no truth to the rumor?" Brown asked.

"Rumors usually aren't true," Rowland said. "That's why they're called rumors."

"But sometimes rumors," Brown said, "have a way of coming up and biting you in the ass."

Rowland pretended to think and then said, "That's so. But where are we going with this?"

"Well," Brown said, sitting back comfortably in his chair, "the Salt Lake City PD is now saying it's a crime scene and the people who were in the room have now been moved to another, less conspicuous room. Do you have anything to tell us?"

"About what?" Rowland demanded, his voice squeaking at the end of the sentence.

"About what happened in that room," Brown stated.

"You're being silly now," Rowland told them.

"I don't think so," Brown said menacingly.

Rowland shifted uncomfortably in his chair and said, "Do I need a lawyer, detective?"

"Why?" Brown asked. "Did you do something wrong?"

Rowland pointed at the door and said, "Why don't you guys get the fuck out of here?"

Brown smiled again and said, "Now, that's the Eddie Rowland I'm familiar with."

Rowland picked up the phone, and Brown said, "You don't need to do that, Eddie. We'll find our own way out." He stood and walked toward the door, with McKenzie—not looking very happy--close at his heels.

When Brown reached the door and had his hand on the knob, he turned back and said, "Oh, by the way, did you ever know someone by the name of Litzy Baker? She was a hooker who used to service you. At least that's the rumor that's been circulating for some time."

Rowland was obviously rattled by the question and said, "Yes, I knew Litzy. Why do you ask?"

"Someone tossed her out a window," Brown said.

"Oh, really?" Rowland responded. "I thought she committed suicide."

"There's another nasty rumor," Brown said. "See you later, Eddie."

And he walked out of the room, followed closely by McKenzie.

When they were gone, Rowland picked up the phone, his hands shaking, and dialed a well-known number.

***

When they got to the car, McKenzie climbed into the passenger seat before Brown could reach the driver's door. Brown squeezed behind the steering wheel, and before he turned on the engine, he looked at McKenzie and asked, "What's been bothering you?"

McKenzie didn't look back as he said, "Did you have to be so hard on him?"

Brown had a look of astonishment on his face when he asked, "Are we showing some empathy toward good old Eddie?"

"Have some respect, man," McKenzie said. "After all, he might be president someday."

Brown said, "Over my dead body," with a look of disdain.

It was then that McKenzie gave him a look that Brown didn't see because he was in the process of starting the car and pulling away from the curb, but the look McKenzie gave him was one of malicious intent.

***

When Hanson got to Rowland's office, they sat together in a huddle, while many individuals waited in the outside office to speak to Rowland as if he was some type of King. Most of them realized that that was what Rowland truly wanted to be; they wouldn't be surprised if he went that route if he was elected, and they were sure they could win a seat beside him if they only did what he asked them to do. They were willing to do whatever it took if they could remain in his good favors.

Hanson told Rowland that the red-haired cop came from a family of conservatives, and he might be the one to approach if the heat got too hot. Rowland was still sweating and hurriedly wiped it away with a large towel before he saw his minions, as he called them. He began to calm down as Hanson explained to him that McKenzie was their ace-in-the-hole; he was sure that McKenzie would go along with them as long as the end result was Rowland's presidency. And they were going to make sure of that if they had their way.

After a considerable time, Rowland's sweating stopped, and he finally allowed the first of his minions to step into his presence. As he dealt out his commands, his minions weren't aware of anything wrong; they were just looking to get their foot in the door of the White House. Rowland dealt fairly with them—or as fairly as he thought possible—but he also got rid of them as fast as he could because he wanted to have some alone time. This was very obvious, for Hanson had seen it many times before, so he unobtrusively slipped out of the office, and Rowland didn't notice anything; he was too wrapped up in himself to notice anything about anybody else.

Rowland sat at his desk in a blue funk. He didn't want anything to go wrong. He now knew he could really be the President of the United States. He had to hold his head up high, especially in public. He was the republican front-runner, and he was going to stay in front because that was where he liked to be. His many adversaries would know his name as he strode forward into the limelight. His many republican competitors would fall by the wayside as he chopped them down and away one by one. No one could defeat him, especially not Julie Borstrand. She had put his whole campaign into motion, and she would soon find out how powerful he had become.

He stood up from his desk, squared his shoulders, and marched out of his office, where he would go upstairs to his penthouse and fuck Carlotta's brains out. She had to know who was master and who was slave. He was surprised, as he rode up in the elevator, how hard he was becoming at the thought of reducing Carlotta to someone who sucked him off at any time he wanted her to obey his needs. The only thing he didn't realize was that Carlotta was conspiring behind his back to take over once they were in the White House. He was an extremely uninformed and useless person. Carlotta knew this, as most people in Rowland's orbit did. They only hung around to get some of the power that was being thrown at Rowland. Carlotta would suck him off and swallow as much of his cum as he wanted in order to attain her place beside him as they entered those golden gates of that massive white house on Pennsylvania Avenue. She knew that Rowland was blinded by sex, so she would do whatever it took to take over.

It was known as the power of the pussy.

So, with Rowland getting his rocks off by shooting his wad into Carlotta's mouth, the campaign continued with debate after debate and Rowland whittling his competition down to practically nothing, except for two hearty renegades who believed that they had enough stamina left in both of their campaigns to bring Rowland down to his knees. Unfortunately, their individual staminas were taken away from them by Rowland's dirty tricks until they were left gasping for air and stranded with the rest of the "losers," as Rowland would describe them.

He was now so puffed up with his own self-importance that he wouldn't respond to any phone calls that didn't benefit him: his focus was entirely on the presidency, and he would not let anyone get in his way. He left the running of his businesses to his children, with, of course, weekly updates because he didn't want his children to know everything about his businesses; they must be kept in the dark about many important things. He ran everything and everyone beneath him with an iron fist.

10

Brown and McKenzie, on the other hand, were working on what had become known between them as "The Eddie Case." McKenzie had wanted to call it "The Mr. Rowland Case," but Brown wouldn't hear of it because his respect for Eddie was nonexistent. But McKenzie was in some kind of a funk about the case, and argued consistently with Brown about dropping it, which was unusual for McKenzie; after all, McKenzie was usually very passive when talking with Brown. If Brown's thoughts hadn't been on other things, he would have realized that McKenzie was making somewhat of a stink about investigating Rowland at all; in fact, if Brown had really thought about it, he would have realized that his partner was sympathetic toward Rowland. But he didn't think about it at all, for his mind was laser-focused on getting the goods on Rowland, who was a disgusting human being in every sense of the word.

So, they continued plodding along, Brown doing his best to get the facts on Rowland, following in his footsteps, realizing that Rowland was a no-good bum, something he had been aware of from the beginning because his father had worked on the construction of the Rowland building. He had been an independent contractor and worked at his own business, and worked very hard for Rowland because he felt he was going to have a big payday when it was over. But Brown's father never got a big payday, nor did the other contractors, because Rowland decided to stiff them instead of making good on his contracts. He was sued by them all, but Rowland just declared bankruptcy under one of his umbrellas, and the cases went away like magic. But Brown's father went into a deep, dark depression because he couldn't pay his bills, and eventually had to declare bankruptcy himself, but he didn't have any other umbrellas to hide under, and the business went bust, and Brown's father died of what some called a broken heart, but Brown knew deep inside himself that his father had been murdered by Rowland. If he could have gotten him for that, he would have done so, but it was beyond his control, so he found something else to vent his spite: the murder of possibly two women by Rowland himself. He rubbed his hands with glee when he thought about it.

McKenzie's blue funk had started when they began the investigation of Rowland. Brown didn't notice, of course, and McKenzie's adversity to what they were doing only fueled Brown's endeavors to jail Rowland even more. McKenzie tried valiantly to sidetrack the investigation as much as he could, but Brown was too devoted to ruining Rowland's life to notice.

McKenzie was still living with his parents, so every night as they sat around the dinner table, he would discuss what he and Brown had done that day, which only made his father mad as hell and his mother weeping silently, for she felt that the world was going to hell in a hand basket and they needed Rowland to save them.

McKenzie tended to agree with his parents. When in college, he had joined the Young Republican's League, where he learned from many young conservatives that the Jews had taken over the world and they needed to be wiped out. McKenzie didn't know if that meant killing the Jews, but he sort of agreed with the theory. For as long as he could remember, the Jews ran New York City; that is why Jesse Jackson called Manhattan "Hymie Town," angering the many Jews who lived there, which made his job harder than ever. If they could take over Manhattan, McKenzie thought, why not the rest of the world?

He was thinking these thoughts as Brown made phone call after phone call, trying to nail down Rowland's movements for the past couple of months. McKenzie was on his computer checking his e-mails when something popped up that he hadn't expected. It wasn't an ad of any kind, but it was intriguing; although the return e-mail was not available, the offer to speak with him about his investigations into the activities of Edward Rowland surprised him no end. He wasn't sure if he should respond, but he couldn't help reading it over and over and over again until his eyeballs were ready to pop out of his skull. He looked furtively around him to make sure no one could see the e-mail, especially not his partner. He saw that Brown was still on the phone, angrily making demands of someone on the other end of the line. McKenzie shook his head as he thought of how Brown wanted desperately to pin something on Rowland. McKenzie needed to do something about it, so he returned to the e-mail and wrote a response to what he considered to be a mysterious and somewhat mystifying missive from someone who didn't want to reveal himself. At least, not yet. They agreed to meet that night at a little known pub across from Washington Square; it was very popular with the students from NYU, so there should be nothing dangerous, but if there is, McKenzie thought, I'll have my Glock with me. After all, he should see what all the mystery was about. Should he tell Brown? The e-mail said not to, so he wouldn't. Obviously, whoever wrote the e-mail already knew a lot about him and his professional life. So, he'd keep it simple. He didn't like keeping secrets from Brown, but he'd already kept the secret that he was a republican. I'm sure that would surprise Brown if he ever found out, and probably it would cause a rift between them, so he would not say a word about it to anyone. It is dangerous to discuss politics nowadays, especially in this political climate. As they say on the news constantly, the country is badly divided, so it was better to keep one's mouth shut, and that included discussing it with your partner on the NYPD. He was good at keeping secrets, this one in particular. So, he kept to himself as long as the investigation into Rowland kept on its "merry" way. McKenzie looked over his shoulder to make sure Brown was still on his phone. He was, so McKenzie turned back to his computer and answered the e-mail.

Brown was still on the phone, trying to lock down Rowland's steps that led up to the murder of a very young hooker. The only problem was that the hotel had told him that Rowland had checked out the day before the murder took place. It was obvious then that Rowland's gang had paid the hotel staff off, and the hotel staff had made sure the computer would say just what they wanted it to say. Brown banged down the phone in frustration, and when he did so, a number of the detectives at their desks looked up sharply, including McKenzie. A few of them made some smart remarks, and there was a moment when the detectives playfully teased each other. But it passed quickly, and everyone went back to their jobs, except for McKenzie, who looked over his shoulder worriedly, keeping tabs on his partner.

Just as McKenzie wasn't sharing any information with Brown, so Brown was keeping a lot to himself, and McKenzie could feel it. Maybe Brown was suspicious of him after all and didn't want to make things worse by telling McKenzie what he knew, even when Brown really didn't know anything that would put Rowland behind bars. But McKenzie didn't know that, just as Brown didn't know that McKenzie would be conspiring behind his back. So, the pair of them worked independently of each other, and were not able to come together as the partners they should have been.

12

So, as the days and weeks went by, Rowland did more to insult his enemies than any potential president before him, using language that usually did not come out of the mouths of politicians. But then again, Rowland wasn't a politician, he was a dirty businessman, with all that went with that. He was as corrupt as they made them. He ran his corporation as a Don would run his organization. He treated his employees with disdain, but he paid them well, so they stuck around and did not complain. He was high on the list of rich men, but he didn't have as much money as he claimed. He was a malignant narcissist who thought only of himself and no one else, and that included his children. He treated them as playthings, especially Priscilla, whom he had fucked when she was 14. She didn't protest at the time, only laid back like a limp doll and accepted her fate. They never fucked again, but she sucked him off a number of times, because then she was in total control, and she liked it that way. The first time she had done it, she spit out his cum, but then she swallowed it every other time, enjoying the taste of her father. She never reported him, neither to the police nor her mother. She thought of him as a disgusting pig, but he was still her father, and she showed him the proper respect, even if it was laced with contempt.

His sons, on the other hand, were conspiring behind their father's back. They wanted the Rowland empire to be theirs for the taking. They wanted their father to either die or be put in a home somewhere. After all, he was becoming more and more senile by the moment. They could see it in his eyes. Eddie Rowland was regressing, slipping into his second childhood, becoming hard to handle. Therefore, they felt it was up to them to make sure the Rowland empire remained theirs and not slip into someone else's hands, while their father slipped away.

They needed to usurp his power before it was too late. They needed to take over by sliding their father further away. Then the two sons would battle it out between themselves. Only the strongest would survive, but nobody knew who the strongest was. Everyone outside the family considered them both weak, and that would never change. Rowland considered them both weak, and he would never turn over his empire to them. It was all meant for the oldest child, Priscilla, and that would never change either. However, the two brothers were looking at the throne enviously and were already thinking of how to get rid of the other. And then there was Priscilla. There would come a time when she would definitely need to be unseated. There would come a time when they would need to do that. But that was far in the future, and they would already be getting their talons ready.

13

Detective McKenzie had already met with his secret e-mail "admirer." And plans were being made should Detective Brown ever get close to nailing Rowland. One would think that the partner of a detective would have some scruples when it came to getting rid of his other half, but McKenzie was unscrupulous in many ways, and that even came to politics. He followed Brown around wherever he went and did not interfere with his investigation. He simply listened to what was being said and repeated it back to his e-mail "admirer." Wherever it went from there, he was not interested. Besides, he already knew where it was going and really didn't care. All he knew was he was taking care of business, and his father would be very proud of him.

Detective Brown, on the other hand, had become so focused on putting Rowland in some kind of prison that he did not notice much else around him. His eyes were focused on the prize, and he wouldn't give up until he had achieved his purpose. For the time being, he tolerated McKenzie by his side, but for the most part, he worked alone, his mind situated on his intention, which was to crucify Rowland if he could. He had hated Rowland for some time now, seeing him for what he really was: a fraud. His real estate empire was a sham, and he would continue to enforce his rule until he had everyone in New York City under his thumb; that's also what he intended for the country. Brown could see this. There were many others who saw what he was up to, but, unfortunately, the United States was inhabited by many stupid people, he thought, who did what they were told, and many of these morons worshipped the bullshit that was Rowland.

Meanwhile, Rowland was flying from destination to destination on his private jet, greeting and shaking hands with his worshippers, standing up in front of them declaring that he was the only one who was running for president who could fix the problem. Of course, he never told them what the problem was that he was going to fix. He also stood before them and used the most vile language because he knew that his fans—who were primarily poor white trash—used the same kind of language. They laughed every time he said something smarmy or uncalled-for or simply did not belong in a political candidate's mouth. He presented himself as a man of the people, so he spoke like one to the delight of many morons in the crowd. The Republican Party just stood and shook its head, not quite sure about what was happening.

His wife, Carlotta, was conspiring with all her might with Maria, her personal assistant, about taking over the White House after Eddie became president. It was exciting to both of them, and they talked and giggled behind Rowland's back. That was exciting in itself, for Rowland was an out-and-out demagogue, who Carlotta was going to unseat.

"It'll be so simple," Maria said, "just keep sucking his cock for him, that'll win him over."

Carlotta was sure Maria was right, and therefore gave Rowland his nightly blowjob, which left him with a big, contented smile on his face. Did he ever think about satisfying me? she thought. No, she concluded, he was far too selfish for that. She didn't mind sucking Rowland off, if it meant he wouldn't have to put his shriveled dick inside of her, which she was grateful for. She used to have a boy toy who chaperoned her around town and fucked her in the back of her husband's limousine; the chauffeur had been well-paid to keep his mouth shut. But those days were over, she would now have to be a loving wife in order to become First Lady, then the ruler of the United States, then the world. It sounded insane, as any rational person would tell her, but she now felt, after talking with Maria many times, that it was certainly a possibility.

Not too long afterwards, Carlotta Rowland was found dead in her bed, apparently having died in her sleep of some unknown cause. The police heard of it, and Brown and McKenzie were on the scene within the half-hour. Carlotta looked as if she had been laid out in her coffin already, serene and beautiful, not a mark on her. She was so young, Brown thought, as he looked at her corpse, reveling at how natural she looked, the words someone who was looking at her in her coffin would say. McKenzie stood steadfastly by his side, not looking at the body, not looking at his partner, just looking into space. Brown asked a few questions of the coroner on the scene, but the young woman by the name of Emily Wilmington had no answers to give him; she said that it seemed to be a natural death, but the only way to make sure was by opening her up and looking inside. Brown asked if there would be an autopsy. Emily said only if the family asked for it, but since the death was non-violent, there was no need for one.

Brown decided to ask some questions of Eddie, who was out in the living room, sitting on the couch, weeping copious tears, pretending to be grief-stricken, Brown thought as he watched him; maybe they were glycerin tears, or Rowland had an onion buried in his handkerchief. McKenzie tried to keep Brown away from Rowland, but Brown wouldn't be interfered with. He approached Rowland as if he was a linebacker charging after the quarterback in a semi-final game. All the others in the room were surprised at the way in which Detective Brown questioned Rowland. Besides, this wasn't a homicide, so what the fuck was he doing there? He was showing no compassion toward Rowland; he was acting as if Rowland was not one of the victims but instead was a murderer. If only they knew the truth, Brown thought, as he waded through their accusing eyes.

The questioning went nowhere, so Brown left the premises in frustration, followed by McKenzie, who wore a small smile on his freckled face, a smile he hoped no one would see. Rowland looked after them, wondering when they would go away, much as many people in New York wondered when Rowland would go away, and for good. But Rowland didn't know this, all he knew was that he was now rid of Carlotta who had been conspiring against him with Maria, that bitch who always had it in for him. If it wouldn't look too crazy, he would have had Maria taken out as well. The tears he was shedding were not exactly crocodile tears, for he would miss Carlotta's nightly blowjobs, but he was glad to be rid of her after the long battle they'd had two nights before. It took him that long to set up her demise, and when it was over, he felt a great sense of relief.

He had come into her bedroom unexpectedly (he was usually not allowed in her bedroom; she usually came to him to suck him off) and he overheard her on the phone to Maria, plotting to take him down once he was in the White House. He stood there in the doorway, dumbfounded, the light from the hallway spilling onto her bed, just barely touching her. Then, she noticed the light and abruptly turned in Rowland's direction. The old expression, "If looks could kill," sprang from his face, and she was suddenly scared. She ended her call abruptly, and Rowland stood still, his hands bunched into fists, ready to take her by force and fuck her brains out until she died with his hard cock still inside her. But he knew instinctively that that wasn't feasible, so he moved slowly into the room and closed the door behind him.

After a knock-down, drag-out fight in which they called each other names that they had never called each other before, he actually slapped her, and she fell backwards on the bed and didn't move. He leaned over her and could feel her breath through her open mouth; he knew she was still alive, but not for long, he thought. So, he made a call to the man with the gravelly voice— his "fixer"—and the man came over as quickly as he could—for Rowland paid him a lot of money for his expertise—with a doctor's bag in his hand, and once he was inside the bedroom, he took out a syringe filled with a certain liquid that would put her to sleep for good. As soon as he had injected her in a spot that would not be noticeable, he returned the syringe to his bag, and, without another word, picked up his very professional bag and left the bedroom and the master suite of the Rowland building, and traveled by elevator to the lobby, where he left through the lobby doors into the street and disappeared into the night. No one approached him or spoke with him, for if they had, they would have realized he was not the doctor type.

Rowland remained on the couch, still weeping crocodile tears and looking at the crowd that the bedroom of his dead wife Carlotta had attracted, from below just barely lowered eyelids, while the NYPD and the mortuary assistants looked over Carlotta's body to make sure it was not an act of violence. Aside from the bruise that appeared on her cheek, they could find no other signs of violence, and the bruise could have been anything she might have done to herself while sleeping. So, they ruled the death as a natural one, and the mortuary assistants agreed and bundled the body of Carlotta Rowland into one of those black bags and put her on a stretcher and took her to the morgue, where she would be cremated as soon as possible at the behest of Edward "Eddie" Rowland himself. It was done and accomplished within the next two hours. (Not surprisingly, for those in the know, Maria, handling her grief well over the loss of Carlotta Rowland, and thinking of ways to get rid of Eddie Rowland, for she knew he was responsible for Carlotta's death, stumbled while walking down Fifth Avenue and fell into the path of a quickly moving cab and was thrown at least twenty feet into the air and came crashing down on the cement sidewalk, a mass of crushed bones and torn flesh. No one there seemed to notice the lanky man with the gravelly voice as he disappeared into the crowd, and the cab that had hit her was never found, unless one was willing to search the bottom of the Hudson River.)

Meanwhile, Detective Brown figured that the string of deaths connected to Eddie Rowland were no accidents. He needed to prove beyond a doubt that Eddie Rowland was a megalomaniac who wanted to win at any cost. Therefore, not only was he a recent politician campaigning for president, but he was also a cold-blooded murderer. Sure, he hadn't wielded any weapon, but he gave the orders, and that was just as good as pulling the trigger of the gun that had killed Mike

Espinoza. If only he could prove it, which was becoming more and more difficult. But Brown moved forward, trying his best to find the evidence that would put Rowland behind bars forever, disregarding the threats aimed at him by his captain, who wanted him to take care of his other cases instead of wallowing in the cesspool that was Eddie Rowland.

Brown, however, had become so totally obsessed with Eddie Rowland that it was almost impossible for him to investigate anything else. His focus was skewed to the point of obscurity; he was no longer his own man.

One night, not too long after the death of Carlotta Rowland, Brown unexpectedly appeared on the doorstep of Detective McKenzie's condo he shared with his parents. They were in the middle of dinner, and Brown showed no courtesy at having interrupted them. Instead, he sat at the table with them and discussed his endeavors to find Eddie Rowland guilty of several murders, while McKenzie's father, a large red-haired and red-faced man in his early sixties, drank more whiskey and fumed silently, hoping Brown would go away before he quietly snuffed him out of existence for looking for ways of putting his idol behind bars.

McKenzie knew that all this was going on inside of his father and laughed quietly to himself, but really, he also wanted Brown to leave before something unforeseen happened to his partner. McKenzie's mother sat quietly, withdrawn and unhappy, for she was frightened of her husband and did not want the night to go along in such a way that they would all regret it sooner or later.

After Brown had stumbled out into the night, for McKenzie's father had shared his bottle with him, McKenzie and his father argued throughout the night, while his mother slunk away to her bedroom, for her husband and she did not share a bedroom any longer, and the two men drank some more and grew sloppily drunk and made the difficult way to their bedrooms after two o'clock in the morning.

McKenzie was not looking forward to the hangover that awaited him in the morning as he fell asleep shortly after his head hit the pillow.

***

The next morning, before he went to work, his head pounding with the force of a jackhammer, he put in a call to his contact from the Republican Party, who had called him some time before to ask him to give him updates on the investigation being conducted by his partner. After a while, while sitting at his desk in the squad room and noticing the emptiness of his partner's desk as unobtrusively as he could, his captain came to him and asked if he had heard from Brown at all that day. McKenzie admitted that he had not, but would check in on where he might be. After making a few what he knew were futile calls to Brown's cell phone, he told his captain that he would run over to Brown's apartment to make sure he was all right. The captain told him to wait until the afternoon because it was too early to send out an alarm.

When the afternoon came, McKenzie told the captain that he was going for lunch. The captain told him to check out Brown's place afterwards because the fact that he hadn't shown up for work yet and had not called in, and was not answering his phone, was worrying. So, McKenzie had a quick lunch at the deli down the street from the station house. When he was done, he almost literally skipped to Brown's apartment, where he knew what he would find. And sure enough, it was as he had imagined it.

There was no answer to his knock on the door, so he got the manager of the building, flashed his badge, and asked to be let into Brown's apartment, or he would be forced to break down the door. The manager grabbed his keys and hurriedly complied, rushing up the stairs ahead of McKenzie and nervously slid the master key into the lock and turned it without much success at first.

McKenzie had to take over opening the door, and when he walked in the smell of cordite and blood filled the air. McKenzie asked the manager to wait outside, which the manager did obligingly.

What McKenzie found was not very surprising to him, for Brown lay on his sofa, his head against the wall behind it, his eyes with a surprised look that almost made McKenzie laugh, and his service revolver on the floor at his feet, with Brown's blood splashed on the wall from the large hole in the back of his head; he was seemingly a victim of suicide. McKenzie thought "seemingly" for he knew the truth of the matter, but would not say a word about it, for he had put the wheels of the murder into motion and obviously did not want to be found out.

After McKenzie put in a call to the station, he did his best to calm the manager down before looking around the apartment to make sure nothing was evident about the truth of the situation.

When the other detectives and uniformed cops arrived, he explained to them what he'd found, and then the forensics team showed up, with the coroner close behind, and they started working on the scene, while the detectives waited in the hall outside the apartment and shot the shit and joked and laughed, in spite of the fact that one of them was lying dead inside the apartment. But, if truth be told, they didn't like Brown, primarily because he was black. Racism in the NYPD was well-known among the officers and administration, but no one seemed to care or do anything about it.

A few hours went by before they wrapped up the scene by carting Brown's body away on a gurney. Fortunately, there was an elevator in the building, so they didn't have to take the stairs, and when outside they lifted the gurney into the coroner's van and drove away. McKenzie looked after the van with the sense of a job well done, and he especially did not feel any guilt whatsoever, for he had taken care of a problem that would have been an insufferable bore if Brown had been allowed to live. As the days went by, Brown's death was termed a "suicide" (the reason given was that he was so obsessed by the Rowland case that he became extremely depressed by the lack of evidence), and the case was quickly closed. McKenzie remained, unfortunately, untouched, and he moved on up in the department. His father was very proud of him. His mother, after the night spent with Brown in the comfort of their home, did not know what to say or do.

***

Meanwhile, down on the ranch, Rowland continued to eliminate his competition by humiliating them in front of the television audience, so that they eventually stepped down and left their campaigns, unfortunate remainders of a war where there was only one winner; he was proving himself to be such a pig, Julie Borstrand felt, and she continued to think this as the days and weeks and months continued to crawl closer to the conventions. He was going to be the republican nominee; she was sure of that. Then, what would happen? Nobody could possibly answer that convincingly.

The republican convention arrived, and among all the hoopla and grandstanding, Rowland was voted to be the nominee on the first ballot, to great and resounding nonsensical applause. The unexpected death of his wife only made him that much more electable: the grieving widower. He was introduced to the crowd by his daughter, who smiled a lot and turned when her father came on the stage and met him halfway to the podium, where he put his hands on her hips, unlike anything a father should do, and tried to kiss her on the lips, but she turned her face away and he kissed her on the cheek instead. The look of disappointment on his face was so great that many in the crowd and many who were watching it on television noticed and were nauseated because they knew what a great letch he was, even with his own child. He disgusted many people, including many Christians, but they still reached out to him and praised him as a great man and wanted him to be a great president.

When he got to the podium, he delivered an address that he felt would put the fear of god into his supporters, even though he did not believe in god and only wanted everything for himself and his friends and his relatives. While his supporters reached out to him, he reached out to Wall Street and welcomed the rich into his arms, where they would grow richer. He promised that he would clean the streets of the disgusting filth that went on everyday and turn the horrors around us into brightness and daylight. And the people with no common sense believed in him, but those who did not awakened the next day into a beautiful dawn and a beautiful day that did not reflect any of the rhetoric he espoused.

The weeks went by, and Rowland continued his wrongheaded rallies and swore over and over that he would pay for his supporters fines if they should be arrested because of what he expected them to do, which was to attack the liberals around them and make them pay for what they had done to this country. He used the term "liberal" as Joe McCarthy had used the term "communist." In fact, Rowland was just as big a demagogue as McCarthy had been, but his supporters did not realize this or did not care, for they were so swept up in the furor that surrounded Rowland they wouldn't have cared one way or the other if they had known. All they seemed to want now was someone in the White House who would clean up the "swamp" and make it so they would not have to be ashamed of what the country stood for. What they didn't know was that Rowland wanted to turn the USA into an authoritarian country, devoid of any feeling for the allies that stood behind the country. He was a great admirer of Hitler, and so he was prepared to turn the country into a pale reminder of Nazi Germany. And the first thing he did was tear down the media so that his supporters would not trust anyone but the "journalists" of Fox News. In spite of the fact that Fox News was proven to be full of lies and full of liars, Rowland's supporters listened to and believed every word that passed through their lips.

Actually, the world was going mad. Authoritarianism was becoming a part of almost every industrialized country. Sinclair Lewis had once written a novel called It Can't Happen Here; he wrote it while Nazi Germany was trying to take over the world, but it seemed to happen all over the globe now. Far right groups were coming out of the shadows and threatening the liberties we had always believed in. The people around the globe were voting for authoritarian figures in frightening numbers. America seemed to be the last bastion of democracy, but that seemed to be quickly fading away, and those with any sort of common sense were terrified. They tried to fight against the aggression that was looming over everyone's head, but the fight was not leading to anything constructive. Instead, the world was losing its mind with every step the far right was taking. We were about to face inestimable doom if something wasn't done about it. And very soon.

However, that didn't seem to stop the world from revolving, or the people from moving in directions that would eventually kill off the human race. There were those who scoffed at the idea of climate change, the anti-vaxxers were coming out in droves to warn people off cures that would save their lives, and the bullies of the world were uniting to push the little man around because it made their egos feel good. And the lead bully was Edward "Eddie" Rowland, the dumbest fascist and most incompetent politician to ever run for the presidency. There are those who are known to be prophetic, and there are those who are known to be dimwits. Unfortunately, the dimwits seemed to be winning. And they were voting for their leaders who wanted to quash them into submission without realizing they were doing so.

14

Julie Borstrand became the democratic nominee easily, and the night they met on the debate stage was a night to remember. It was more of a boxing match than a debate, for the way in which Rowland circled Julie around the stage was more than antagonistic, it was demonic. He had a look of pure evil on his face, and his fists were clenched tightly as if to deliver a deadly blow, and he huffed and he puffed as if he wanted to blow the house down with Julie in it. Julie ignored him, which some thought was not a good thing to have done. He circled her menacingly, and some thought she should have addressed the situation in one way or another, but Julie's strategy was to stand firm and proud in the midst of all his vainglory. Her supporters were very proud of her and felt she won the debate, but Rowland's supporters tore her apart, saying in essence that she was a cold fish and not able to be president, when in fact she was one of the most capable candidates who had ever run.

After the debate, Julie returned home to her apartment in Manhattan rather than go to the party that had been planned at her campaign headquarters. She paced her bedroom and realized, if she hadn't already, that Rowland was becoming more of a problem than she had thought he ever would be. In her mind, he was an impertinent usurper who suddenly realized he could become president after all and ruin her original plan because he wanted the power that went along with the job, and he would ruin her if need be in order to climb to the very top of the world. Unfortunately, it wouldn't blow up in his face as it had for Jimmy Cagney in the gangster movie "White Heat," but what many people didn't understand was that Rowland was himself a gangster, maybe not as brutal as Cagney had been but close to it.

So, the days wore on, until the big day came, the first Tuesday in November, the day when all the bets were on the table, the day when gamblers near and far put their money on the particular person they thought would win the presidential election. The candidates went out and placed their own votes, then greeted their supporters with all the hokum and bluster that was expected of them.

As the day wore on, the people streamed in and out of the polling places and voted for their choice for president. David Lopez, owner of the Mole, sat behind his desk and watched the activity on Fox News and declined to take part in it, for he did not believe in voting for a person who did not fit all the requirements he expected of them, so why bother? He'd rather sit behind his desk, smoking his cigars and drinking his whiskey and getting drunk until the bar closed, then he would get up from behind his desk and order his car to be brought around and when it arrived, he would lumber out the front door and into the back seat and the driver would take him home.

Herb Rinaldi, detective from the 49th precinct, felt it his civic duty to vote, for his grandparents had been immigrants fresh off the boat from Italy and went through the process on Ellis Island which was the first step to becoming citizens of what they felt was the greatest country in the world. Because of that, Herb was a diehard proponent of everything American. His grandparents came over here for a better life and they had wanted their descendants to achieve great things. Of course, Herb had ascended to the role of police detective, and that might not have been the success his grandparents were looking for, but it fit Herb just fine. He wished his grandparents had been alive to see when he received his gold shield, an achievement of greatness that he would have loved to share with them.

Joaquin, bartender at an after hours club on the Lower East Side, watched the television up in the corner as he wiped glasses clean with a small rag that had seen better days. He thought about voting, but was unsure as to who to vote for. He thought Rowland was a chump, but he liked some of his ideas, while Julie Borstrand was no president as far as he could tell, for he didn't think a woman should run the country. Women were good for only two things, cooking and fucking, and that was it. They had no right to be in the White House; they were too emotional to run a country such as this.

And he wasn't alone in such thinking, for Jackson Blue, former boyfriend and roommate of Litzy Baker, had felt for a long time that women were only good for spreading their legs and accepting the seed of men, nothing more. While Nancy Evans, the former next door neighbor of Litzy Baker, wished for a woman to win, because then the country might grow instead of regressing. Rowland wanted to take the country back into the 1950s, before Civil Rights; he wanted to send all the Black people back to Africa and all the Jews to Israel. He wanted to make America all white again, even if he never came right out and said it. So, she walked into her polling place with her head held high and voted for Julie Borstrand, which she felt was the right thing to do.

Jake Gottlieb, former lover of Mike Figueroa, watched his television as he slowly but surely committed suicide with booze and pills, which he had been stockpiling for many years now for just this purpose: he thought the world would be coming to an end soon, and besides, he had been unable to shrug off the death of Mike in which he had been complicit and had suffered in his heart. Two or three days later, they found his body, and it was soon to be rotting completely.

Al Hanson, longtime friend and campaign manager of Eddie Rowland, walked into the polling place and came out with a sticky note on his coat declaring that he had voted. He knew that he had done his civic duty and was proud of himself. He had also done as much as he could have for Eddie, and now, they would wait an agonizing day or more to find out the results. The Rowland children—Priscilla, Daniel, and Roger—went to the polling place on Fifth Avenue and voted for their father together. They came out as a team, and the paparazzi took their photos for the newspapers they worked for. McKenzie, former partner of Ted Brown, came out of the polling place around the corner from where he lived after having voted for

Rowland and let out a contented sigh.

Carl Van Schneider, medical examiner, was too busy cutting up bodies to vote; maybe he would do it later. Adam Feldman, husband of Priscilla Rowland, voted for his father-in-law with some misgivings; he was aware that Rowland was anti-Semitic, and the only reason that he allowed Adam and Priscilla to marry was because Adam was so far from a Jew that it seemed to please him. Now, he could say he wasn't anti-Semitic because his son-in-law was a Jew, a blatant lie that satisfied no one.

Terry Wainwright, managing editor of The Tribune, watched the news with a cynicism that knew no bounds; he found the government of the United States to be ludicrous and untruthful. Politicians preached unity and togetherness, when in fact they never believed a word they were saying, especially the republicans, who were greedy and ruthless; the reason they were first called conservative was because all they really cared about was conserving their money, and to hell with everyone else.

Wainwright admitted it to himself and tried to put it in his paper as often as he could. As far as he was concerned, republicans were the axis of evil that George W. Bush called those outside of the White House. He once said, "If you're not with us, you're against us," as if there was no other alternative. Wainwright knew that that wasn't democracy, it was authoritarianism. Such thoughts resounded in his head with a fury that chilled him right down to the bone.

Connor Binghamton, the Irish mob boss, had his henchmen vote for Rowland, and they were instructed to vote for Eddie Rowland because he knew that Rowland, a thug himself, would take care of them and let them continue in their nefarious schemes. The captain of the 49th precinct mourned Detective Brown's "suicide" for a minute, then it was business as usual; he had no desire to vote, but he knew that when he got home, his wife would insist they go out and do their civic duties. Miss Stanhope, Rowland's buxom secretary, was hoping she could give her boss a celebratory blowjob when the news of his victory filtered in; she was too wet at the thought of it to go out and vote.

So, the day wore on, and the voting continued, and when the polls closed that night, they waited for the results. They came in slowly but surely; the electoral results showed that Julie Borstrand was in the lead. This infuriated Rowland, and he screamed and shouted and threw things. Then, unexpectedly, everything turned around and Rowland surged in the polls. This infuriated Julie Borstrand, and she cried bitter tears when alone; she didn't want to show any weakness to her supporters. While Rowland cheered and shouted happy things, this time. The counting of votes continued into the night, but Julie was never in the lead again. Rowland was ahead and never looked back. His supporters cheered for him after every state was declared.

Finally, the night ended, and Rowland was declared the victor. Julie Borstrand made her concession speech, and then, she disappeared from view, locked in her room and sobbing away, while her husband tried to console her from outside the locked door. The skies darkened, and rain began to fall for days. Uncle Sam and the Statue of Liberty embraced and wept bitter and copious tears. The night was Rowland's. He beamed, as proud as a peacock. He stood tall and erect, his head held high, his heart full of venom. He climbed to the dais that had been put up in his campaign headquarters for his victory speech. The television cameras were aimed at the spot where he would stand in front of the microphones. His supporters waited expectantly until he appeared, then, when they saw him approaching, they screamed in anticipation. Rowland faced them, with his cruel smile lighting up his rather plain, ugly face. He stood in front of the microphones, looking down on the people who had helped him win the election, and he felt such hatred for them; if asked about it, he would have been unable to explain it. In the stance he assumed, he looked very much like the dictator of Italy during WWII, Benito Mussolini; he was just as pompous, and his thoughts ran to how and when he would crush the people. After a while, he leaned forward toward the microphones, and the evil that resided in his heart began to speak.

The End